MW00619861

SING, BARREN WOMAN

YOU ARE DESTINED FOR PURPOSE

LINDA DAVISON DODSON

ISBN 978-1-7376371-0-3
Ebook ISBN 978-1-7376371-1-0

Cover design by: Amy Renée Design • www.amyrenee.design
Layout & Interior design: Amy Renée Design • www.amyrenee.design
Music and Korean consultant: Jinho Choi, Composer, JC Score
Interior Photographs: Jinho Choi, Linda Davison Dodson,
Tim Dodson, Don Ferguson, NJ Photography, and Cathy Wood
Gaylord House Illustration: Tom Allen
Published in the United States of America by Amazon

Library of Congress Cataloging-in-Publication Data
Names: Davison Dodson, Linda, author.
Title: Sing, Barren Woman — You Are Destined for Purpose
Subjects: Infertility, Childlessness, Fruitfulness, Supernatural Intervention, Destiny,
Purpose, Living Intentionally, Fulfilled Dreams, Missionaries, South Korea, Dream Sparker

Thank you, Jesus,

Because, all my life, you have been faithful.

I love you,
Linda

🎵

Song: *"Goodness of God," by Jenn Johnson, Bethel Music*

With Thanks

To my beloved parents, Darrol Davison and Mary Lou Jones:
Thank you for loving me and giving me a wonderful life.
I have missed you both dearly. You were the best!

To my special "Other Mother," Glenda Davison, and "Other
Fathers," Edward P. "Brud" Jones, Jr., and Paul Wycoff: You did
not bring me into this world, but you loved me as your own. I
appreciate your prayerful support and the gift of each one of you.

To Tim Dodson: Thank you for your love through the years. You
cheered me on as I dreamed and aspired, even when it stretched
you to do so. You have been supportive and wise.

To all my family and friends: Thank you for your love, laughter,
phone calls, and prayers. You enthusiastically joined me on my
adventures and blessed my life by just being YOU. You are some of
my greatest treasures and have enriched my life beyond measure.

Thanks to Jinho Choi, Frank Kresen, Amy Miller, Paige Norfleet,
Derene Schultz, and Liz Reinke for reading my book manuscript
and sharing your discernment and expertise.

Last, but not least, thanks to Jinho, my loving, precious gift
from God; 사랑해요. Thank you for meeting me at the Incheon
International Airport in South Korea. It has been a glorious ride —
here's to more of *la dolce vita*. 고맙습니다!

❤ *With all my heart, Linda*

INTRODUCTION & REMEMBRANCE

While walking in the woods one morning at a retreat center in the fall of 1980, I met the lovely Laurel Lee. During our brief trailside conversation, she noticed I was carrying my journal. I learned she was also a writer. Laurel invited me to attend her writing class that afternoon, and I happily accepted her invitation. I joined a small group of writers gathered around a table in a sunlit grove of trees, with my journal and pen in hand.

When Laurel began speaking, I quickly realized she was more than just a writing teacher. She was a captivating storyteller and a brave young woman who had survived terminal Hodgkin's disease when she was only twenty-nine years old. Her heroic story is featured in her book Walking Through the Fire. Defying her doctor's predictions, Laurel beat her disease and delivered the baby girl she faithfully carried during her life-threatening battle with cancer. The book and a CBS movie about her story propelled her into worldwide traveling, fame, and adventure.

A gentle breeze blew through the trees overhead, sending needles onto our table as Laurel dropped inspirational gems about writing and life into my heart. She was an overcomer who effectively wielded her pen and testimony like mighty swords. I hung on her every word. Laurel spread an assortment of cards on the table and engaged us in a simple, but meaningful, writing exercise. She invited us to write a note to someone we thought needed to be encouraged, comforted, or appreciated. To be sure that our cards would get mailed, she even provided us with "LOVE" stamps. Laurel smiled as we each read our card out loud. We all witnessed the power of our pen. The afternoon was bright and full of life, and so was Laurel Lee.

We were asked to bring a sample of our writing to class.

I bravely handed her my personal journal, since it was the only thing of that sort that I had with me. As she read each one's writing, Laurel gave us private, positive feedback. She validated the gift of each writer's "voice" and what she thought made our writing unique. Many times, I have reflected on Laurel's words to me: "You have a lovely writing style that is full of heart. You are like a little house with all its doors and windows wide open. Keep them open, and keep writing." My time with her that day was a gift.

In my relationships and in my writing, I have aimed to be genuine. I was honest, yet private. When I felt nudged, or when something seemed important, I bravely shared my vulnerabilities. I struggled and was imperfect, and I was mostly willing to say so. As a person of faith, I was truthful about my sincere doubts and my unresolved questions. I had seen the value in a personal testimony and shared my stories, hoping they might help others along the way. Yesterday, I smiled inside when a friend said that I was authentic and real.

I recently learned that Laurel Lee passed away in 2004, at only fifty-eight, from complications of late-stage pancreatic cancer. When she was diagnosed with the fatal disease, she was given only three months to live. At the time, she was writing her final book, Tapestry: The Journey of Laurel Lee. Shortly after her diagnosis, she contacted Lighthouse Trails Publishing in Silverton, Oregon. The publishing company rushed to get her book into print while she was still alive. Thankfully, they were able to release her book just one month before the day of her passing. When I heard the sad news, I went to my computer and ordered a copy. I am glad Laurel's beautiful book was published. She poured her heart onto every page.

Thank you, Laurel Lee, for encouraging me as a woman and a writer. Like you, I walked through some fires and slayed some of my own giants. You were abandoned in the middle of your battle with cancer, but you defeated Hodgkin's disease, and your heart eventually healed. As a fellow writer, your encouraging words were forever in my heart. I did keep writing. My pen and my journal have been trustworthy allies. I am happy to have met you, Laurel Lee. We will meet again, Mighty Warrior.

None of us knows for sure how many days we have in this life. As we live and breathe, there will be challenges to face, lessons to learn, adventures to embark upon, and stories to tell. This book is a collection of stories about my journey through barrenness, to a surprising life of fruitfulness and fulfilled dreams. I have sprinkled some favorite songs and videos throughout the book for you to enjoy. Just as Laurel encouraged me to, I have kept my doors and windows open as I wrote. You are welcome to come inside.

Linda Dodson
May 9, 2021 | Albany, Oregon

Sing, Barren Woman

CONTENTS

CONTENTS

CONTENTS

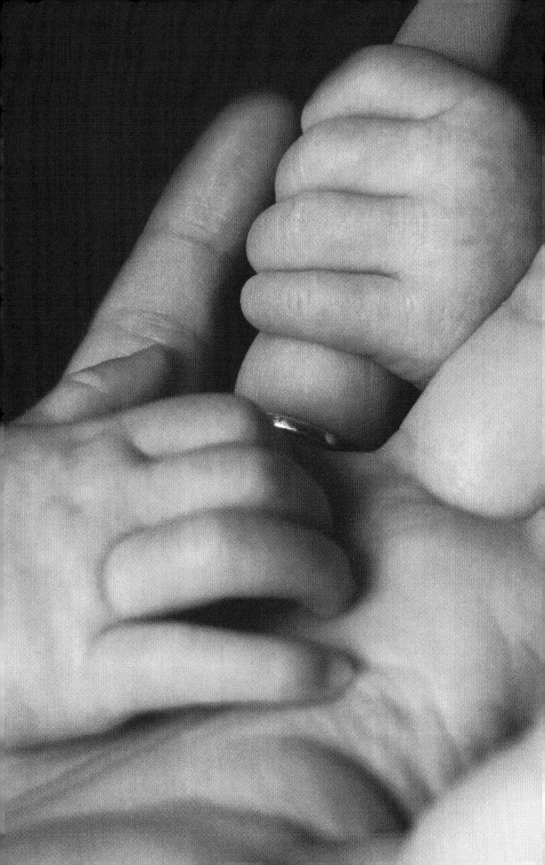

SCENE 1:
MY EARLY YEARS

In the beginning, life gave me about the best start a first child could hope for — loving parents, good health, and a happy family life. My mom created a comfortable home for us and loved me well. My dad was my buddy and a man who was passionate about his career in aviation. I always expected to one day grow up and have a family that would enjoy the same good life I had known.

1.
DREAMS REALLY
DO COME TRUE

My dad always said I was the child of his who wanted life like a big, beautiful package with a pretty pink bow on top. I confess, I always have been an idealist, a dreamer, and one who saw the world through rose-colored glasses. I loved beautiful movies with inspiring, violin-filled scores. And I mostly preferred happy endings, please. Like other optimists did, I saw the glass as half full. I am a dreamer who envisioned the "what ifs" and the potential in people and situations. I know that many of you have been dreamers, too. As John Lennon sang in his song "Imagine:"

"You may say I'm a dreamer/But I'm not the only one."
—John Lennon

I have always liked spending time in the company of other dreamers, "possibility thinkers," and positive, "can-do" people. I became bored and impatient around negative people with doom-and-gloom attitudes. It was not always easy being an idealist, especially when life hurled its snowballs of reality at my face, but I would not have chosen to live any other way. This is who I am. Even my blood type is A+.

I love the paintings of Norman Rockwell (1894-1978), one of America's most-admired artists. I like the way he used warmth and humor, paint and paper, to tell the story of the American dream, even in the worst of times, like during the Great Depression of the 1930s. His paintings portrayed happy, nostalgic images that expressed the idealism and beauty of this life. He brought hope to people in troubled times and left behind a body of work that makes us all, if only for a few moments while looking at one of his paintings, imagine how lovely it would be to live in a Norman Rockwell world.

While gazing at a Rockwell painting, listening to a favorite musical composition, or sharing warm moments with another, I have experienced some of the sublime beauty in this world. I am thankful for those times. Most of us, however, have not lived in a continually blissful state, where perfection and harmony were always present and all of one's dreams really did come true. Regardless of the realities I suffered and endured, I always believed in the power of dreams, the enjoyment of pursuing them, and the satisfaction of achieving them. I always wanted to inspire other people to imagine and reach for their dreams, too.

In my quest to live happily, peacefully, and beautifully, I've had plenty of setbacks, crushed hopes, and disappointments. I can now see that the pain I experienced enlarged my heart and gave me a greater love and compassion for others. My hope is that, as you journey through the pages of this book, you will find new strength to face your challenges and pursue your dreams. I believe that your passion and courage will reap unexpected rewards for you in your life.

I assure you right here, at the beginning of my story, that it does have a happy ending, and so can yours. Somewhere over the rainbow, dreams really do come true.

Song: *"Somewhere Over the Rainbow," by Eva Cassidy*

2.
LIFE IN
REDWOOD CITY

I was privileged to grow up in Redwood City, California — where life was quintessentially Americana, and it was very good. There was a slogan arch over the main street into my town that read, "Redwood City — Climate Best by Government Test." When my paternal grandfather traveled from Nebraska to California seeking a sign for the best place to settle his family, it was the arch's slogan that sealed the deal and moved him there. His decision would also mean that I would eventually grow up in Redwood City, too.

My city, next to the San Francisco Bay, was a great place to live, work, and play. I freely rode my green Schwinn bicycle all over town and felt comfortable walking to school alone and selling my Girl Scout cookies and calendars door to door. Our moms did not have to worry about us kids. They often ushered us outside as they said, "Go play." We were happy, and we felt safe. The "Baby Boomers" kept the movie theatres, roller-skating rinks, record stores, community swimming pool, and ice cream shops in business. Thankfully, in my town, there was no such thing as a school shooting.

The First Methodist Church was where my parents dedicated me when I was a baby. I invited Jesus into my heart in Mrs. Love's Sunday school class when I was just four-and-a-half years old.

Mommy told me that on Christmas I cried when I reported to her, "It was Jesus's birthday today, and we didn't even have a cake or sing 'Happy Birthday' to him." Every Sunday, Daddy and I stood together singing hymns in church, and I sang Christmas carols in front of the congregation when I was only eight. I remember worshipping with a child-like faith when I was barely tall enough to see over the back of the church pew.

I have many happy family memories. As a first child, I was privileged to arrive when my mommy and daddy were building a life together. When daddy's career in aviation was just taking off, they built a small two-bedroom home on Stanley Street. He constructed some impressive rock walls around the front lawn and back patio that are still standing, decades later. Mommy often wore sweatshirts and work pants as she weeded, filled nail holes with putty, and cared for me. I remember her giggling when daddy walked by and pinched her on the fanny. I am glad I was part of their early years in the 1950s, when my parents were creating a happy home and modeling the joys and successes of teamwork. My childhood experience was a positive one. I wanted that kind of family life when I got married, had children, and became a mom.

My childhood fun times were a combination of imaginary girly play, creative projects, and boyish adventures. I climbed huge California oak trees and went "box sliding" down Motorcycle Hill on long, dry grass with large pieces of cardboard curled up over my toes. The creek behind our house invited risky play. I walked across underwater walls in up-to-my-ankles water that threatened to pull me into the deep pools below. I maneuvered my tennis shoes on slippery trails and caught frogs and tadpoles in tin pails. My neighborhood adventures were perfect for my tomboy side. I loved playing in the large trees, picking orange poppies on the hillside, and

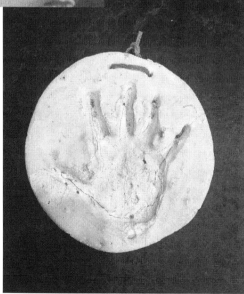

hiding in the tall grass until mommy called me in for dinner. Those were "the good ole' days."

When I was not riding my bike around the neighborhood, playing baseball with the boys, or dangerously climbing Hanley's Rock, I spent time with my dolls, schoolbooks, and art. Daddy built us the cutest little yellow playhouse in our backyard at 1570 Cordilleras Road; it had a Dutch door in its front façade. Inside there were cabinets for art supplies and counters for painting and craft projects. To this day, our playhouse is still standing and looking cute.

Next to our house, there was a pretty grove of silver dollar eucalyptus trees. The ground was covered with a clover-like plant that had a firm stem and a bright yellow flower on top — we called it "sour grass." I would spread out a blanket for my dolly and me. While I sat on my blanket, I decorated the space around me with flower bouquets and storybooks as I chewed on the lemony sour grass. It was my time for playing "mommy" when I imagined my someday baby.

I grew up in the country, just a short bike ride from the center of town. In those days, most families had two parents, and there were plenty of kids to play with. When we got home from school, the front doors were unlocked, and moms were usually there to greet us. Families helped one another, and neighborhood pals shared toys. When our parents gathered to play cards and talk, mostly about boring stuff, we kids played baseball, kick the can, and hide-and-go-seek outside. We did not watch much television in those days, and there were no computers, video games, or cell phones. It was a time for neighborhood play and youthful freedom. The post-WWII years were full of hope and optimism for most American families. It was a good time for idealistic dreamers like me to grow up in.

Both of my parents were artistic and wonderfully supportive of my creative interests. They bought the supplies I needed and encouraged my art, ballet, writing, dance skating, and music. My creative stash included paints, colored pencils, journals for writing, fabric for sewing, a Betty Crocker children's cookbook for kitchen play, a folk guitar, dance roller skates, a high-fidelity record player, and 45 rpm and 33-1/3 rpm vinyl records. A favorite musical memory is the night my father returned from New York City with the Meet the Beatles album. "Yeah, yeah, yeah," my girlfriends and I all squealed with delight over John, Paul, George, and Ringo, the "Fab Four."

My generation grew up during the "Golden Age of Travel," when aviation was rapidly developing. I was fortunate to be part of an airline family who had free flying privileges. In the early days of traveling by air, it was company policy for employees and their family members to dress in their best clothes while flying on free passes as "non-revenue passengers." Our cross-country airplane trips were super adventures in themselves. I felt fortunate to have opportunities to travel and be exposed to interesting places and people.

My mom and dad were great role models. They made many sacrifices to provide us with a good life. They created great childhood memories and wanted the best for their kids. We felt loved. I wanted to be just like them when I grew up and had children of my own.

I appreciated my mom's great care. When I was a young girl, she polished my little white Buster Brown shoes every night. Though she once told me she was far too critical of me as I was growing up, I figured she did her best. And she was much wiser than I ever gave her credit for, especially during my teenage years. As my twenties approached, I decided to move out on my own. It seemed like time to become my own person and not who I perceived others wanted me to be. So, at nineteen years old, I moved from Connecticut back to California, the state of my birth, and did not live in my parents' home again after that.

I did not do life perfectly on my own, but I matured as I learned to support myself. I was thankful my dad had encouraged me to study business in high school and learn to type and take shorthand. I was free to find my own way in the world and to imagine the future I wanted to have. I was blessed with Catherine and Rebecca, two close friends to journey through my teenage years with. My aspirations were to travel, write, and someday get married and be a mother. I wanted to be the kind of mom who would lovingly champion her children as they pursued their dreams. I always needed a few people in my life to champion me.

A Story From My Teenage Years

After my San Carlos High School graduation in 1966, my father accepted a position at the corporate offices of American Airlines in New York City. It was a great opportunity for him, so our family relocated from California to Old Greenwich, Connecticut. The East Coast was much different and more formal than was the relaxed West Coast where I grew up. But New England provided unique experiences and a good life, too.

While at American Airlines, dad worked on special projects with Korean Airlines and made several trips to Seoul and Pusan, South Korea. One night, he brought home a 33-1/3 rpm record of Korean music. Included on the album was one of the Korean people's favorite folk songs, Arirang. I was intrigued with the song and learned that Arirang originated in Jeongseon, Gangwon Province. There were 3,600 variations and sixty versions of the beloved song. According to the legend, the name was derived from the story of a bachelor and a maiden who fell in love while picking camellia blossoms near the wharf at Auraji (아우라지). Dad asked me to learn the song and play it on my guitar for a special guest who was coming to our house for dinner.

Not speaking Korean, I listened to the song many times and used my high school shorthand skills to transcribe it phonetically. The evening came when our special dinner guest arrived; he was Mr. Choong-hoon Cho, the President of Korean Airlines. After dinner, my sister and I sang Arirang for Mr. Cho. He got tears in his eyes as he listened to our performance and kindly said we did a very good job singing in Korean. When we were performing for Mr. Cho, we did not know that Arirang was sung by a nation who longed to be transported from pain to hope as they lived a hard life of poverty. Every Korean knows the song, and, when they sing it, they often cry. For sixty years, Korea was one of the poorest countries in the world but transformed itself from a farming to an industrialized country. The song represents the spirit of their nation.

I could not have imagined that someday I would visit the very country our special guest was from, and the same cities my father had visited. Perhaps a Korean seed was planted in me that night as my sister and I sang for Mr. Cho.

Song: "*The Story of Arirang*"

Song: "*So Hyang — Arirang Alone*" | 소향 – 아리랑 *[Immortal Songs 2].*

SCENE 2:
MY JOURNEY
INTO INFERTILITY

"Sometimes to get your life back,
you have to face the death of what
you thought your life would look like."

— Lysa Terkeurst

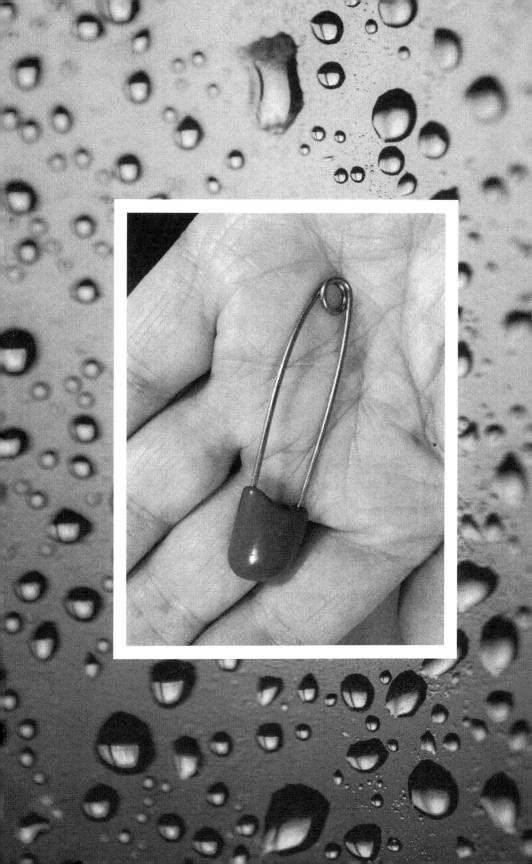

3.
DOUBTS
AND DELAYS

I am the firstborn child in my family. I shared a happy life with my sister, Sherri, who is four and a half years younger, and my brother, Randy, who was born in 1957 when I was nine. I enjoyed new babies arriving and being a little mother to my siblings. I was my mom's first diaper changer, babysitter, and driver. Motherhood and family life were what I always wanted. I imagined that one day I would be a happy mother of children living in a country house surrounded by flower gardens. I never planned to have an ambitious career. I had no "Plan B" for motherhood. That was what I always wanted and had pictured for my life.

When I was an idealistic, young twenty-four-year-old, I got married in 1972 in the garden of an old estate wearing a wreath of flowers in my hair. I planned to live happily ever after. Unfortunately, the marriage experienced unhappy times and separations. Because the future of my first marriage felt uncertain, I thought I needed to use reliable birth control. I did not want to bring a precious baby into an already unstable marriage. Remember, I had always pictured myself as part of a happy family enjoying a "Norman Rockwell life."

In the 1970s, I chose "The Pill" for my birth-control method, but the public became concerned about its health risks. The original pill was a much stronger version of the one a woman takes these days. I had many serious side effects from the pill and researched a better option to prevent pregnancy. From 1970 to 1974, a doctor and an engineer had developed and released a new, non-chemical method of birth control called the "Dalkon Shield." It was an intrauterine device (IUD) that was reported to be ninety-nine percent effective at preventing pregnancy. At my doctor's advice, I chose this new, presumably safer form of birth control, as did 2.5 million women in the United States, 1.7 million women in foreign countries, and approximately 4.5 million women worldwide.

After a challenging seven-year marriage, in 1979 the relationship ended in divorce. My dream of a happy married life was shattered. I spent precious time working toward reconciliation, even after our divorce was final, but my efforts were unsuccessful. I was back at square one, single and broken-hearted. I had spent some of my prime, fertile years in a marriage that ended in divorce. The death of my marriage also brought my motherhood dreams to a halt. It was a devastating finale.

In 1982, when I was thirty-four, I married again — to Tim, a man who also wanted children, though he already had a son from his first marriage. When we were dating, I saw a cute photograph of him lying on a couch with his two young nieces tucked under his arms. He looked like a man who would make a good daddy for the children I hoped to have.

In our first year of marriage, we decided to start a family, but, for the first several months, I did not get pregnant. One day, our pastor came to visit. While he was at our house, he found a diaper pin lying on our living room floor. I had never seen that diaper pin before and still have no idea where it came from. With a smile on his face, he handed me the pin and said, "You are going to have a baby soon."

I felt excited and encouraged. I thought the diaper pin he placed in my hand must surely be a sign of good things to come! When I was unable to conceive, however, my dream of being a mother felt threatened again.

Months later, I was still not pregnant, so I scheduled an appointment with a gynecologist and hoped he could help determine the cause of my infertility. On appointment day, I stepped into the world of medical testing and diagnosis, another childless woman seeking the answers to the "whys," with fear in my mind and heart. I left the doctor's office with my first homework assignment: monitor and record my ovulation (fertility) cycle. Having a plan of action gave me some hope.

For several months, I took my basal body temperature each morning before getting out of bed. As directed, I recorded the data onto little hand-drawn charts that I kept in my nightstand drawer. The paper charts, with their dots and lines, revealed my fertility cycle and the best days to get pregnant. My husband and I paid attention to the "good days," when my fertility was at its peak. Though I felt somewhat optimistic, my emotions and marriage also became burdened with having sex on the best days. My fertility cycle took precedence. Infertility robbed me of spontaneity because I sometimes focused more on making a baby than making love. When our attempts to get pregnant were unsuccessful, I experienced more disappointment.

On a follow-up visit to my gynecologist, step two was recommended: an exploratory dye test called a "hysterosalpingogram" (HSG). At the hospital, dye was injected into my uterus. It was supposed to flow into and immediately out of my fallopian tubes. The test revealed the worst possible news. Both of my tubes were blocked. My doctor's best guess was that the blockages were probably caused by the pelvic inflammatory disease (PID) I had years before when I used the IUD.

The IUD became known for causing infections that led to fallopian tube scarring and blockages. There was a string attached to the IUD, so that a woman or her doctor could check to see if the device was still in place. They later thought that the string probably wicked bacteria into a woman's uterus and fallopian tubes, which led to infection, sepsis, miscarriage, injury, and even death. My medical records documented that I was treated for two cases of PID. Some women reported that their IUD had imbedded itself in their uterine wall and had to be surgically removed. Even though I'd had mine removed years before, the damage it left behind remained.

I was stunned by the devastating news that the pathways between my ovaries and my uterus were blocked, which prevented fertilization and gave me no chance of becoming pregnant. I was a new wife that dreamed of a happy marriage and family life. My gynecologist discussed several possible scenarios, and some were quite scary. He was optimistic that he could surgically open my tubes and that I could get pregnant.

In my pre-surgery appointment, my doctor said he might find cancer. I knew it was standard procedure for him to discuss all the possible causes of my blocked fallopian tubes. Doctors need to disclose accurate information and protect themselves from future liabilities. It was unsettling to see the photographs in his medical journals and hear about the possible causes I had not even considered. I scheduled my operation and hoped for a successful surgery, even as I prayed for my baby.

I left my appointment that day feeling more unsettled as the unknowns and "what ifs" occupied my head. My chance for motherhood felt threatened. In addition to coping with my infertility, a fear of cancer was added to my list of concerns. As a woman, I began to feel defective, like damaged goods. My world was shaken, and my peace left me. Uncertainty demanded that my prayers and faith go to a deeper place.

One August morning in 1983, the second year of our marriage, I had a salpingostomy to repair my blocked fallopian tubes. My surgery was first on the operating room schedule. When I was wheeled into the pre-op room, I was comforted to see the masked face of my friend Gloria, an RN from my church. In her sweet, soothing voice, she calmed my pre-surgery jitters and assured me that I would be in good hands.

Surgeons have crazy-demanding jobs and work long days in intense operating-room environments. Dr. Tom performed multiple surgeries that day. As I waited and wondered, it was an uncertain, faith-stretching day. The 7:30 a.m. surgery lasted three-and-one-half hours, but I waited all day for a post-op report. My doctor came to see me at 10:00 p.m. with the news that both of my fallopian tubes were completely blocked. His good news was that he was able to surgically open them.

One tube had a pea-sized piece of scar tissue blocking the tube. He cut the tube in half, removed the blockage, and sewed it back together. The other tube was closed at the end. All the "fingers" designed to pull the egg into the tube were stuck together, and the tube had begun to balloon up. He cut that tube open and snipped new fingers on the end. He said, "Overall, the surgery was successful." He was encouraging and hopeful that I could get pregnant soon. I felt cautiously optimistic and thought, That was a pretty good report.

When I left the hospital two days later, I felt thankful. I wanted to celebrate my successful surgery by making a faith purchase. I asked Tim to drive me to the local children's shop downtown. After looking around, I chose a white baby dress with delicate pink flowers and green leaves embroidered on its neckline. Thinking it would be the perfect little dress for my baby girl to wear on her dedication day, I made my purchase. I liked the girl names "Rebecca" and "Isabella."

Many people prayed for the baby girl we both wanted. In the months following my surgery, friends gave me faith-filled gifts: little dresses, a soft, pink teddy bear, baby shoes, and a rattle with a rainbow on it, the symbol of hope and promise. Their gifts were full of love, and I was happy and expectant. I confidently believed for my fertility and eventually for a baby. My family and friends echoed the same belief and positive expectations.

I lovingly wrapped my baby girl's dress in pink tissue paper, placed it in a little white box, and put it in my cedar hope chest. Occasionally, I took the box out and opened it. As I held the sweet dress, I imagined how adorable my little girl would look wearing it. I prayed for my baby girl and for myself. Other times, I cried. Some tears flowed from a thankful heart for my successful surgery. Other crying was triggered by the weariness and pain I endured as I waited for my motherhood longings to be fulfilled. I was confronted by the fear of not knowing when or if the little girl I wanted would come.

> *Uncertainty was a difficult place.*
> *I didn't want to stay there.*
> *It was a place where faith told me,*
> *"Move beyond the tears and fears, and just trust."*

—*Linda Dodson*

4.
LIFE MOVED ON

One year later in 1984, I still was not pregnant. My husband accepted a new position, and we moved from Corvallis, Oregon, to San Ramon, California, close to San Francisco. We left our first home, where our pastor had handed me the diaper pin and said I was going to have a baby soon. We said "Goodbye" to friends and family and the doctor who had helped me weather my first infertility storm. It was difficult to leave, but Oregon was in a recession, and we needed work.

Our new jobs in California involved joining a team for the start-up of an engineering company. Tim worked as a civil engineer, and I was an administrative assistant, typing engineering reports and organizing company events. Our fellow employees in the growing company were like family. We settled into a cute rental house and were thankful for steady jobs and being able to live where the economy was booming. We were busy with work and new relationships as we waited for our family to begin.

Unfortunately, when infertility persisted, my doctor suggested I return to Oregon for a second dye test. I feared what the test might reveal, but I decided I would rather deal with the known than continue to live with the unknown. I scheduled an appointment and made my trip north for the procedure. The results of the retest confirmed my worst fears. One tube was completely blocked. The other tube was minimally open. When the doctor applied pressure on the instrument, only a tiny stream of dye flowed out. Fallopian tubes are quite delicate and smaller than a straw. During the healing process, scar tissue can form and cause the tubes to become blocked again. It was not the conclusion I had prayed for. I needed my mom that afternoon, but she was 3,000 miles away.

For months, tears came in waves. Infertility was a huge blow to my heart and to my womanly identity. Disappointment caused a part of my heart to begin shutting down. I felt emotionally numb. I wanted a miraculous healing. Others had faith and prayed for me when I wrestled with doubt. I considered having a second tubal surgery, but my doctor did not expect a better final outcome. It was a tough time that I somehow managed to get through.

During the next few years, we had consultations with fertility specialists in California. Since both of my fallopian tubes were blocked, the pathway to fertilization was totally cut off. There was zero chance of my eggs being fertilized by my husband's sperm. At that point, a glass petri-dish attempt was my only hope for egg fertilization and possibly motherhood. An in-vitro fertilization (IVF) specialist offered a high-cost option that had a low success rate; neither of those statistics worked for me. We also did not have the $20,000 they quoted to take a chance on an IVF procedure that offered only a ten percent chance of pregnancy. I had never been a gambler, and frankly, I wondered how many more hope-disappointment cycles my heart could bear. I reached the time when I just wanted to be freed from the emotional ups and downs of infertility's roller coaster. It was not a fun ride.

Following the devastating results of my second dye test, I battled depression and a loss of vision for my life. Infertility was a giant hammer that smashed my hopes and dreams. Though my internal struggles were not obvious to those around me, my anguish was deep and intense. The tender, nine-inch scar at my bikini line was a constant reminder of my deficient condition.

"A heartbreak isn't always as loud as a bomb exploding.
Sometimes it could be as quiet as a feather falling
And the most painful thing is…nobody hears it except you."
— Unknown

I turned again to medical professionals hoping they could help me through my first serious bout with depression. The doctor's only idea was to treat my emotional pain with an anti-depressant medication — a "mood elevator," he called it. Feeling at an all-time low, I decided to give his suggested remedy a try. Though I was never much of a pill taker, I surrendered my unstable emotions to the doctor's prescription. In hindsight, I think a combination of journaling, being part of an infertility support group, and talking with trained counselors would have been much better options for my barren heart.

I tried taking the "happy pills" the doctor thought could help me, but the medication only dumbed me down and transformed me into a chemically altered emotional person. A thick fog settled over my life. I felt a loss of my true self, whoever she once was. The medication brought me no peace. I actually experienced more inner turmoil. A couple months later, I threw the not-so-happy pills in the garbage and never returned to an anti-depressant "solution" again. What I really needed was to exchange the uncertainty caused by my infertility for peace and hope for my future. But that shift had not yet taken place. I experienced that the way up was often first down.

5.
A FUTURE
AND A HOPE

Through the years and tears following my infertility diagnosis, I did my best to regain the optimistic outlook I had lost. There was uncertainty surrounding my future, making it hard to stay at rest and trust. I had to exercise my faith every twenty-eight days when my menstruation came again. My monthly hormones only intensified my already-sensitive emotions. That is when I often asked the question, "Who am I?" Infertility caused me to question my identity and my entire life path. I kept hoping that I would finally get pregnant. Yet my hope was continually denied. My fears were like thieves that showed up every month to steal my destiny.

"The thief comes only to steal kill and destroy;
I have come that they may have life, and have it to the full."
— John 10:10

I referred to this period of my life as my "fog-bank years," because I could not see where I was going. Where I once had a clear vision of how I thought my life was going to look, infertility had erased my picture. Life lost its color. I experienced the loss of my past and future dreams. There are no funerals for the death of a vision. I silently grieved the pain of preparing my heart and life for the child who never came.

Part of my ongoing struggle was the sadness and doubt that I battled. My peace was repeatedly threatened. Sometimes, I had faith; at other times, I felt overcome by grief. Looking back at my journey, I can see that I began to feel deadness inside; perhaps it was my way of coping with the heartache of my infertility — my survival mode. Infertility brought a depression that was sometimes referred to as an "emotional hangover," when it seemed like I had nothing left to give in the midst of an extremely traumatic period.

There are stretches of time that I still have little or no memory of. As a woman of faith, I began to wonder if my God was even aware of my desires or not? Could I continue to trust Him, no matter what the outcome of my journey as an infertile woman might be? My faith and mental health were tested more than once. Maintaining an attitude of trust was often just a decision — not something I actually felt.

In the meantime, I decided to look for a job. It seemed like time to get myself out among people. This, too, required me taking deliberate steps. I looked for creative work opportunities, and, as I did, I found it helped me to refocus on loving and serving others. I was able to redirect my attention to a life outside my own skin and emotions. It was a less self-centered, healthier place to live. I also needed to get off my hope-disappointment-hope-disappointment roller coaster ride. It was only my faith that sustained me in those days, as I pursued the answer to the BIG question, "Why was I born?"

American author Mark Twain (1835-1910) said:

> *"The two most important days in your life are:*
> *1) The day you are born and*
> *2) The day you find out why."*

We are all on a quest to know why we are here and to fulfill our "Why?" Where I once had no vision or hope for my future, I was eventually able to trust, even when life's circumstances opposed my optimism. When I needed the strength to carry on, it came. Even though I did not receive my miracle baby, I believed my future was in good hands. In the middle of my emotional struggle, I sensed that happier days were ahead. The greatest miracle was that I did not give up on life. In spite of my unfulfilled dreams, I continued to walk forward into my uncertain future.

For many years, my emotions were up and down as I waited and yearned for my miracle baby. I began to feel I needed a deadline, a specific time when I would quit hoping I would get pregnant. More than once, I experienced the deferred hope that makes the heart feel sick. Statistics showed that babies born to women older than forty had a greater risk of having birth defects. I decided that, for me, my fortieth birthday would be the time I should probably surrender my desire for a child. Regarding reproductive fertility, time was not my friend. My "Big 40" deadline was quickly approaching.

A part of me still believed, however, that eventually my testimony could also be like that of Abraham and Sarah in the Bible, who, when she was ninety-one years old, finally birthed their promised son, Isaac. (I also recently read that in 2019, a seventy-three-year-old woman in India named Erramatti Mangayamma, gave birth to healthy twin girls and fulfilled her lifelong desire to be a mother! Hmmmmm; reading her story made me pause.) Honestly, I never stopped believing that even though test results showed that my fallopian tubes were blocked, still, it was not impossible for them to miraculously open and my wish for a baby to be granted, no matter what my age was. Perhaps I watched too many Disney movies, with their "they-lived-happily-ever-after" endings, when I was a little girl.

I have always looked for a happy ending, or at least the silver lining in clouds.

To the husbands of precious infertile women: Your women may feel, as I did, that they are the cause of your dreams to have a son or daughter not coming true. They need to know that no matter what the outcome is, you will still love them. To the spouses and friends of these barren women: You can lend your faith and speak encouragement to them. You can be the bridge between their doubt and their destiny.

My husband and I briefly considered adopting, but our financial and emotional resources to invest in the expensive adoption option were limited. For many infertile couples, I thought adoption was a wonderful decision. I respected the birth mothers who had lovingly and unselfishly chosen to release their babies for adoption. I greatly admired adoptive parents who made room in their hearts and lives for the children they did not birth. I personally knew unselfish couples who agreed to "open adoptions," so that the birth mothers could stay connected to their children and also become part of the new family. I had heard many wonderful testimonies of adoptees whose lives were blessed with love and the wonderful opportunities they might not have otherwise had. God bless all the adopters and adoptees.

"I didn't give you the gift of life. Life gave me the gift of you."
— Anonymous Adoptive Parent

The idea of adopting felt too risky for my already-grieving heart. It was hard to know when to hope and when to let go and accept my childlessness. Even though it was a challenging time, I always had a glimmer of hope. My hope was not in an outcome; it was anchored in my faith. I was confronted with this question month after month and year after year: "Can I really trust and rejoice in this disappointing situation?" I continually decided that my answer was, "Yes, I can choose to trust."

As my faith was tested and I maintained an attitude of thankfulness, I proved to myself that I had passed my tests — well, most of them. Ultimately, I entrusted my heart and my life to the One I placed my faith in. It was a humbling time. Infertility was a constant reminder that I was not able to fix myself. Thankfully, choosing to trust allowed me to become better, not bitter, and to grow in faith. In the elevator of life, I pushed the "up" button and did not allow my feelings of self-pity to overwhelm me and send me to the basement. I fought back my feelings of being overwhelmed and sang through my tears.

Song: "The Prayer," by Andrea Bocelli and Katharine McPhee

6.
LIFE BEGINS
AT 40

My desire to be a mother was the longing of my heart for nearly two decades. After enduring my long season of disappointments and heartache, the time came to seek meaningful substitutes for my vanishing dream. I had to accept that my baby might not be coming — not then, and, probably, not ever.

At the age of forty, while browsing in a boutique, I spotted a button that read: "Life Begins at 40." Its hopeful message resonated with my spirit, and I felt an encouraging comfort wrap around my heart. This simple declaration seemed like my new truth. I bought the button and stuck it in my bulletin board at home, where I saw it every day and considered its message. My dream of motherhood had slipped through my heart like sand in an hourglass. I fought back the doubt and depression that tried to sneak back in. As I considered my life and waited, "Help me to trust you," was the prayer continually on my lips.

"I've tried my best, but if today I lose my hope, please remind
me that Your plans may be better than my dreams."
— Unknown

As I longed to be a mommy, I heard about the horrible atrocities against children all over the world. I was grieved about the escalating abortion rate, the heinous act of sex trafficking, and the heart-wrenching stories of child abuse. I questioned why some people were even allowed to be parents. Why did abusers get to have children and I did not? I knew I would have provided them with a loving home and a happy life. There were no satisfying answers to my difficult "Why?" questions. Looking back, it seemed miraculous to me that I continued to believe that life could go on, no matter how messy, unfair, and unjust things were. When I trusted that someone greater than all of these problems cared about the desires of my heart, I found some comfort. Even though I did not get what I had wanted or expected, I concluded that life could still be good. I persevered instead of giving up.

What would fill my huge baby void? Only time would tell. As I waited and trusted, I tried to keep my rose-colored glasses on. I felt hopeful that, in time, new dreams would surely come.

SCENE 3:
MY SEASON
OF FRUITFULNESS

*However, as it is written: "What no eye has seen, what
no ear has heard, and what no human mind has conceived,
these things God has prepared for those who love him."*
—1 Corinthians 2:9 NIV

Gaylord House
c. 1857

7.
THE BIRTHING OF A
HISTORIC PRESERVATIONIST

After living and working in California for four years, my husband got a new job in Oregon, and in 1988 we returned to the Northwest. It was good to return to our old hometown near family and friends. I had processed a lot of emotions and life experiences during our four years in California. There were both challenging days and good times in "The Golden State." But when we returned to the Northwest, I was still childless, dealing with identity issues, and seeking direction for my life.

The nagging sorrow of infertility was waiting for me back in Oregon. It was probably because I returned to the place where my infertility journey had begun that the old emotions reattached themselves to my heart. I realized that I had to fight for my new, hopeful perspective that "Life Begins at 40." Our relocation gave me the chance to push my "reset" button and start a new chapter in my life. I was definitely ripe for positive changes.

While reading the Corvallis Gazette-Times newspaper one morning, I spotted a small front-page article offering an interesting opportunity. A group of preservationists would be meeting to discuss saving an historical house in town. Unless it could be moved, the Charles Gaylord House, built during Oregon's 1850s-1860s settlement period, would be demolished and lost forever. It was probably the oldest pioneer house in town. An attorney had purchased two city lots on Third Street with a small historic house on each parcel. He planned to have one house torn down, build his new office on that lot, demolish the Gaylord House, and put a parking lot in its place. It was a threat that fit the storyline of Joni Mitchell's song, "Big Yellow Taxi:"

> *"They paved paradise, and put up a parking lot."*
> *— Joni Mitchell*

As I read the article, the plight of the historic house tugged at my heart. I felt a kindred spirit with those who were interested in preserving a significant part of Oregon history. Since I'd just moved back to town, there was a lot of open space on my calendar. I decided to attend the meeting and learn more about the preservation effort. It was a pivotal life decision. As English evangelist Leonard Ravenhill said, "The opportunity of a lifetime must be seized in the lifetime of the opportunity." The passion for preserving history that had been planted in my heart years before was about to be put to good use.

In the late 1960s, I lived with my family in Old Greenwich, Connecticut. I enjoyed traveling around the East Coast of America, so rich in history. That was where my interest in American history and my appreciation for historic architecture was birthed. I enjoyed visits to a local salvage company on the edge of town called "The House Wreckers." It was fun to see the antique parts they had saved from historic buildings slated for demolition. I admired the glass knobs, fireplace mantles, vintage doors, egg-and-dart wood trim, porch columns, Edison-light-bulb fixtures, and the old wooden sleighs they had salvaged. It was quite the collection.

When entire buildings could not be preserved, the House Wreckers disassembled them and salvaged at least some of their architectural parts. What remained of the buildings was later smashed and hauled off to the local dumpsite. Tragically, many historic structures were bulldozed and lost forever. I appreciated knowing that the rescued materials I saw could at least be reused in other projects and be admired by old-house lovers. During my time in New England, the historic preservationist in me was nurtured.

My East Coast sightseeing adventures took me to places like Old Sturbridge Village (a 1770s-1830s recreation of rural New England life), Plymouth Rock (1620), the 17th-century Plymouth pilgrim plantation, Boston, Massachusetts' 19th-century Beacon Hill, and the 19th-century Mystic Seaport Village in New Bedford, Connecticut. Once I walked on cobblestone streets lined with historic buildings, smelled iron being forged in a blacksmith's fire, and sampled cornbread baked colonial-style over an open fire, I was hooked on history. A passion for historic architecture was planted in my heart that would fully blossom two decades later.

At my first "Save-the-Gaylord-House" meeting, Mary, a passionate historian, gave a compelling presentation on the significance of the Charles Gaylord House. Further research later confirmed that the Charles Gaylord House (c. 1857) was indeed the oldest pioneer house in Corvallis, Oregon, from its 1850s-1860s settlement period. My interest in the project was sparked that day.

During the meeting, Larry asked me, "Do you have any small children?" When I timidly replied, "No, I do not," he and several other people in the room laughed. Their light-hearted response pricked the tender spot in my childless heart. I was puzzled and wondered why they all laughed at something that was a source of pain for me. I later learned that Larry and the other members of the Corvallis

Historic Preservation Advisory Board had been discussing the Gaylord House project at an earlier meeting. They had brainstormed about how they might save the house from its fast-approaching demolition. Larry had wisely concluded that what they needed was someone to lead the project that was "new to town, wasn't too busy, and did not have small children at home." He was probing to see if perhaps I was "the one" who might lead the "Save-the-Gaylord-House" effort. Their laughter was simply a display of their positive expectation that, perhaps, I was the person they had hoped for.

After the meeting, I joined the small group who toured the threatened, one-and-a-half story Gaylord House, filled with its wonderful musty, old-house smell and the ambience of its simple pioneer life. It was raining that day, and we noticed water trickling through tiny cracks in the deteriorated wood-shingled roof into the upstairs bedroom. That is when my internal alarm went off! We preservationists knew that moisture and fire were the two biggest enemies of historic buildings, followed by the bulldozer. The humble Gaylord House captured my heart that day, an experience only another preservationist would understand. Somebody has to do something to save this house! I thought to myself. In that moment, I did not know that somebody was about to be me. The opportunity presented itself as a complete surprise.

YOU could be the solution to someone's problem.

That night, I lay in bed listening to the rain and thinking about the leaky roof I had seen. By the next morning, I was sure that I wanted to help rescue the Gaylord House. I jotted down some fundraising ideas and even sketched a letterhead design. I called Rene, the Director of Corvallis Parks and Recreation, who was working with the group, and told him I was interested in supporting their effort. He encouraged me to come to their meeting the following week and share my ideas, and so I did.

When I offered my help at the next meeting, I was enthusiastically invited to be their new leader. I had never imagined taking on such a project. The original group of "Friends of the Gaylord House" pledged their participation and later faithfully delivered on their promise. The multitalented gathering of "friends" included restoration specialists, researchers, grant writers, a newspaper historian, old-house owners, photographers, artists, and lovers of history. They were a group full of passion and talent — a project leader's dream team. There was a skip in my step as I left the meeting that day.

The "Friends of the Gaylord House" eventually grew to more than a hundred dedicated, creative people. With a fast-approaching demolition deadline, we got right to work on the goal of raising $10,000 to move the house to a nearby city park in an historic neighborhood. We sold giant cookies at community concerts and hundreds of hoagie sandwiches at the Fall Festival to raise money and grow our family of "Friends." We received precious donations from businesses and local citizens, some as modest as $1.00. The house's rescue was a heartfelt, grass-roots effort.

In 1989, we saved the Gaylord House from demolition, had it moved just four blocks to Washington Park, and celebrated reaching our successful Phase One goal: The rescue. Then we began Phase Two: The restoration. Larry kicked off the renovation work by replacing the original, rotten foundation beams with new hand-hewn beams made from Douglas fir trees that fell during a timely storm in Avery Park. The "Friends" then made seven "squares" of cedar shingles by hand, about 2,000 in all, for its new roof. The shingles were hand-split with a "mallet" and "froe" and hand-tapered using a "shaving horse" and "drawknives," tools and methods the original pioneer builders would have used. Our project was a pioneering labor of love applauded by State of Oregon preservation aficionados.

When the project began, I knew very little about restoring historic buildings. I just loved them and believed that they should be protected. My passion for preservation compensated for my lack of experience and my limited knowledge. As the restoration progressed, I learned what I needed to know and stayed just a few steps ahead of the process. I was thankful when more capable people joined our team: house movers, Corvallis city officials, engineers, State of Oregon preservation experts, graphic designers, and restoration specialists. Many of the dear seniors who donated their resources and time are no longer living. They made their precious contributions to the Gaylord House before they left us.

I had fun leading an enthusiastic, experienced group of people. More importantly, I was happy I could help preserve a significant part of local history and a pioneer house that I hoped would outlive me. New facets of my own identity were also shaped. Almost a decade of my life was spent saving and restoring the Charles Gaylord House. In the process, I became a devoted preservationist.

As we helped to save and restore the little house, my own heart and life were also rebuilt. My destiny was set on a surprising and exciting new course. The picture of motherhood on the chalkboard of my life, which had been erased years before, began to be replaced with new images. I was still reproductively infertile, but the creativity and productivity of my life definitely became more fruitful. New purpose was being birthed in me.

Where there is no vision, the people perish…
— Proverbs 29:18

Song: *"Be Thou My Vision," by Audrey Assad*

8.
"YOU GOTTA LOVE IT!"

One of my passions has been architecture, especially historic. Leading the effort to save the 1857 Charles Gaylord pioneer house was the beginning of a rich, new season in my life. Through the efforts of many dedicated volunteers, several other historic buildings in my city were also rescued and preserved. I cheered on friends and local citizens as they saved and restored the Willamette Grange #55 (1873), Palestine Church (1882), Willamette Valley and Coast railroad depot (1887), Cumberland Presbyterian Church (1892), Oregon Agricultural College poultry building and incubator house (1907), Sunnyside School (1912), Soap Creek Schoolhouse (1935), and other historic houses.

When I accepted the Mayor's invitation to serve on the Corvallis Historic Preservation Advisory Board, I helped to carry out an Oregon State directive to preserve and protect local history. As a preservationist, I also enjoyed consulting with others and supporting their historic-building projects. My successful restoration projects needed detail-oriented workers who had the necessary sensitivity to the building's original design. The U.S. Department of Interior's "Standards of Rehabilitation" were my go-to guidelines. Restoration work was challenging, but always a joy for me. One of my life mottos was: "You've gotta love it!" I have been privileged to love my work and realize my dream to preserve historic architecture.

"When vision and passion are present, dreams can become a reality!"
— Linda Dodson

As one who always wanted to be a mother, I assumed that I would leave my legacy through my children. I came to realize that, through preserving local history, I could also leave a legacy. I have felt warm joy and thankfulness when I drove by the buildings I helped to rescue and restore. I have hoped that people would continue to enjoy my historic-preservation contributions.

Today, however, was a different experience. I drove to a nearby town to return books to the library. As I approached my right turn, I was shocked and saddened to see a bulldozer, piles of building debris, and a large dumpster occupying the corner where a small (c. 1900) historic house had recently stood. Only weeks before, I had seen a young couple smiling, pointing, and talking as they walked around the turn-of-the-century house. I imagined they were dreaming about fixing it up, because, for a few brief moments, I considered the idea myself when I saw that the house was sitting empty. It happens to me like that — as an automatic heart response, not a logical idea. I saw the house's potential and that its tiny size made it a likely candidate for restoration. Then I noticed bushes being cleared and trees being cut back, as if foundation improvements were about to begin. I anticipated returning in the fall to see that restoration work had begun. I planned to stop by to encourage their preservation project.

Instead, I experienced the disappointment of seeing that another historic house had been demolished and lost forever. Why was there not at least a sign offering a "free-house-you-move-it" alternative? Or did someone at least salvage some of the historic building's materials? Just reducing a historic building to a pile of rubble and throwing it in a dumpster was its worst possible end. I was told that an apartment building was planned for the prominent corner where the cute little house once stood. That news was a big "ouch!"

For many years, I was busy with my job and restoration projects. During that industrious season, my friends were happily raising their children. When their kids got married, I attended weddings as more sons and daughters were added to their families. They became expectant grandparents, and I took gifts to their baby showers. They proudly showed me pictures of their cute grandchildren and told stories about camping adventures and vacations, and also their struggles. Love offered me an opportunity to share in their happiness and just listen. Honestly, though, it was not easy to see others enjoying the family life I had wanted but had been denied.

It was of some consolation that my preservation efforts were appreciated. Old buildings became like my children. My restoration projects were featured in three full-page stories, with colored photos, in local newspapers. I was thankful to have a new purpose and some tales of my own to tell. The day our community celebrated the four-block move of the Gaylord House, the Parks Director surprised me by reading a letter from the Mayor thanking me for my contributions to the preservation of local history. Although it was good to have meaningful projects and creative relationships, I still felt a void in my heart.

Even though I enjoyed my work, I sometimes felt a crying inside about my unmet desire for a child. My accomplishments did not fill my baby void. For me, childlessness was a silent, lonely journey. While my husband was busy with his engineering work, I learned to be content by myself. Meanwhile, my baby girl's dress was still stored in my hope chest, along with other baby items. The desire for her remained in my heart.

For many years, on the second Sunday in May, I was heartsick with the Mother's Day blues. When roses were given out to all the mothers at church, I left empty-handed as a nagging longing consumed my barren heart. Since ten percent of women aged fifteen to forty-four are infertile — currently more than six million in the United States — I knew I was not the only woman in church who suffered from the pain of infertility. Through the years, I wrote a few notes to pastors on Mother's Day that said, "Please do not forget the childless women in your church today. Speak life and hope to them as you celebrate with the other mothers." On some Mother's Days, I just stayed home or took a drive to the coast to process the day privately as I walked along the rhythmically soothing waves on the sandy shore.

To each of you who have suffered the pain of infertility, a miscarriage, a stillborn baby, an abortion, or the death of a child, you know the heartbreak I am talking about. You, too, have felt grief and loss. I have friends and family members who have gone through all of these difficult life experiences. I have pictured your faces as I wrote this section. Please know that you are not alone. Many other women have walked a similar, painful path. We share one another's story.

"With or without a baby, you are valuable, and you matter."
— Unknown

9.
SERVING CHILDREN

On my fortieth birthday, I reached my self-appointed baby deadline. I chose to let go of the baby I wanted so I could embrace the life being offered to me. It was time to let my hopes, not my hurt, dictate my future. Instead of becoming a mother, I thought that perhaps I could be an advocate for the children in my community. I began to consider new possibilities.

When I saw an announcement in my local newspaper, "Seeking a Director for local youth activities center," the job description seemed like a good fit for my interests and abilities. I was one of five candidates who applied. The interview went well, but, in the end, I was not selected. Later, however, I received a phone call from Phil, the Director of the local Boys and Girls Club, who was on the interview panel. He told the others, "If you are not going to hire Linda, I want to." He offered me the position as his Club's first-ever Resource Development Director. After prayerful consideration, I accepted Phil's offer. In the days that followed, I began to feel pregnant with a new purpose. I often sensed when I was on the right track because my mind, naturally and effortlessly, began to think creatively about whatever it was I was feeling guided to do.

As the restoration project director of the Gaylord House, I had contributed to local history and made many special friends in the process. My experiences as a preschool teacher, an Oregon State University newspaper reporter, a fundraiser, and a lover of children all helped to prepare me for my new assignment. Since I had no day-to-day child-raising responsibilities, I was free to volunteer for community-service projects that supported children and families. More fertile fields were added to the landscape of my life. They were not the kind of fields I had ever imagined myself working in, but they were, indeed, fruitful. My new beginning came in my fortieth year. Just as the message on my button had promised me — life began at 40.

Many women who have started careers at a mature age were considered "late bloomers" like I was. Among that talented group were women who made amazing contributions through their art, entrepreneurship, and careers. Their stories are proof that we're never too old to start something new. I would like to honor a few of those women here:

American Folk artist Grandma Moses began painting at the age of seventy-eight, which was a manifestation of her childhood dream. Her father gave young Anna and his sons pieces of white paper that cost him a penny a sheet, because he liked seeing them draw pictures. It was her father's encouragement that fed Anna's passion to paint. As a child, she was inspired through art lessons at school. She used lemon and grape juice, ground ochre, grass, flour paste, slack lime, and sawdust to make colors for her landscape paintings. With no time in her difficult farm life to pursue art, she was obliged to set aside her passion for painting for many years. After raising the five of her ten children who survived infancy, and following the death of her husband at 68, Moses finally began to paint — a total of 1,500 canvasses in three decades!

Grandma Moses' paintings featured no modern amenities and

rejected the rules of basic perspective. They emanated from her lighthearted optimism and the beauty of the rural world she knew. Her simple, old-fashioned, primitive New England panoramic landscapes embodied her version of an idyllic, bygone America. Her works originally sold for $3 to $5 per painting, but as her fame increased, they fetched $8,000 to $10,000 each. The one-room schoolhouse she had attended as Anna Mary Robertson, born in 1860, became Vermont's Bennington Museum and housed the largest collection of her works in the United States.

Grandma Moses won numerous awards and two honorary doctoral degrees and lived to be 101. In his memorial of her, President John F. Kennedy said that her paintings "restored a primitive freshness to our perception of the American scene and helped our nation renew its pioneer heritage and recall its roots in the countryside and on the frontier." Well done, Grandma Moses.

Clothing designer Vera Wang said she believed in "learning and earning her way." She had careers with two of the biggest fashion icons in the industry, Ralph Lauren and Condé Nast, before she launched her own business. When Vera got engaged to be married, at thirty-nine, she had trouble finding a wedding dress. Her businessman father, who did not work in the garment industry, identified that difficult search as an opportunity for Vera. He saw that bridal work came with little risk and a continual stream of potential customers who wanted to be married and needed dresses.

Though Vera says she knew nothing about dress designing, she eventually designed her own wedding dress and had it made at a total cost of $10,000. She did not feel ready to launch her own business but said that her DNA was "to find something I felt passionate about, to make a difference, and to work, and so that is what I did!" Her designs are known for balancing modern style with traditional elegance. Chinese-American immigrant Vera Wang became one of the most prominent designers of bridal gowns in America.

Photojournalist Tsuneko Sasamoto is still alive at 105 years old. At twenty-five, she became the first female photojournalist in Japan. Born in 1914, she earned attention for her photos of pre- and post-war Japan, through her classic images that tell the story of Tokyo and her whole country. Her photographs depicted Japan's dramatic transition from a totalitarian regime to a capitalist-based economic superpower and all the social implications that followed.

This talented and fashionable photographer is one of the incredible centenarians who is still collecting ideas in binders, thinking about the people she wants to meet, and inspiring other women. Her current project is photographing flowers for her work titled Hana Akari, or "Flower Glow," a tribute to her friends who have passed away. Tsuneko's work has been driven by her inborn curiosity. She says, "It's essential to remain positive about life, push yourself, stay aware, and never give up or become lazy."

It is women like these, the late bloomers, self-starters, and sensational centenarians, who inspire and encourage me. I recently bought myself a 100th-birthday card. It has been my goal to live past 100 years of age and to continue creating, enjoying a life of purpose, and inspiring others to do the same. Like these women are, I plan to be a dream sparker for others!

10.
SURPRISES COME

As I waited for life to bring me what I wanted, I was sometimes surprised by what actually came. One fall weekend in 1989, I decided to visit several garage sales. Garage sale shopping was never really my passion, but it seemed like a fun thing to do that Saturday. I planned my route the night before. I rarely got up before my husband, but I drove off early the next morning with my short list of addresses. My last planned stop was at the historic Mountain View Grange #429 in North Corvallis, originally known as the Lewisburg Hall and Warehouse Company.

Being an appreciator of historic buildings and antiques, I thought there might be some treasures waiting for me at the 1911 building. Indeed, there were. I purchased several vintage items that day: two wooden bow-back chairs, a wire dish rack, a white enamel pitcher, and two glass measuring cups with their marks molded, not painted, on their sides — all items that exuded turn-of-the-century charm. When I saw that their coffee pots were for sale, I concluded, If they are selling the coffee pots, they must be moving out.

After purchasing my items, I talked to Dick and several other elderly grange members sitting around the covered front porch. During our conversation, I learned that the members had aged and their number declined. They could not meet expenses and decided to close their grange. There were still vineyards, orchards, and farms in the surrounding area, but families no longer needed their grange hall for a place to socialize with neighbors. Time and modern-day city life had brought change to the social structure of their rural lives. Gathering to discuss how the state legislature could support their life as farmers was also an activity of the past. Once a thriving community hub, the old grange hall and its original purpose had become outdated.

The older gentlemen sitting around the front porch that morning looked quite downhearted. As the people carried off the grange furnishings, I heard one man say, "It's a sad day, such a sad day." His friends agreed, their heads nodding. I saw some teary eyes, too. I felt their grief as I watched them witnessing the final breaths of their beloved community hall. Their melancholy emotions tugged at my heart, but I resisted accepting that their grange had reached its end. As I sat there, I began to envision a brighter future for their special place. I pictured its complete rebirth!

I asked Dick what was going to happen with their building. He said they were considering letting the fire department use it for a practice burn. Oh, no! I immediately thought to myself. They had also talked with the owners of a salvage company, similar to the House Wreckers that I used to visit in Connecticut, whose interest was in disassembling the building to salvage its strong, historic lumber. At that moment, the preservationist in me went on red alert! I was sure there had to be a better future for their community-gathering place than the options they had considered.

I asked if I could go upstairs and look around. They encouraged me to take a self-guided tour of the building. I climbed the stairway to the large, 30-foot by 60-foot second-story meeting room with its twelve-foot-tall ceilings. I saw beyond the worn wood floors, the broken cotton sash ropes and the double-hung wood windows in obvious need of repair, and I caught a glimpse of the building's potential. That is what we preservationists do. We see past the deterioration and years of neglect and are inspired by simple, well-used places that are full of history and shout "Possibilities!" It is our moment of impractical insanity when a seed is planted in our hearts for a place that we are convinced still has potential. We imagine what a building could be. I know, because it happened to me that day as I wandered around the Lewisburg Hall.

A love for the place rose up in me. I had never fallen in love at first sight with a building quite like that before. And the building spoke to me, too. It said: "I have a future. I have a greater purpose. Please do not let them tear me apart or burn me up. Won't you love me and make me beautiful again? I can still make people happy. I promise — I will make you proud!" Yes, I really did hear the building say all those things. I rejected the thought that she could be reduced to a stack of lumber or, worse yet, to a pile of ashes after being burned down. I saw the potential in the old grange, and I was convinced she still had many good years left. This building needs to continue to be a place for the community to meet! I confidently thought to myself.

I headed home from the grange with my newly acquired treasures; a vision for a restoration project was building in me like magma inside an active volcano. Just hours before, when I was waking up to my day, I had no idea what unexpected surprise was about to enter my life. When I returned home, I walked through the front door and enthusiastically announced to my husband, "I found a great old building, and we could even live in it!" When I told him where it was, he looked at me and said "No way! Nobody in their right mind would live in an old warehouse, by the railroad tracks, on the highway."

I did not take offense at him suggesting I was not in my right mind. I was not interested in his quick psychological evaluation of me. "Please catch the vision," I pleaded silently to myself. I asked him if he would go see the building with me. I told him about the older gentlemen who were sitting around the front porch reminiscing and looking sad. Fortunately, Tim does not miss many opportunities to meet and talk with people, so he agreed to go take a look. We were about to walk into my new project — and we didn't know it yet. Well, honestly, I hoped he might also catch a vision of what Lewisburg Hall could become.

When Tim entered the building, wisdom said, "Just let him look around, and don't say a word." I was enthusiastic, but he had already expressed his initial negative reaction — his "INR," as we have sometimes called it. Being an idealist and a visionary, I admit that sometimes I just see possibilities! I don't have to work at envisioning — seeing usually comes easily for me. My husband is an engineer and a practical man. He processes ideas logically. I just kept quiet and did not express what was effervescing on my insides.

As we toured the building, Tim pointed out some of its defects: the outdated heating system, broken windowpanes, old plumbing, and sloping floors, just to name a few of its obvious imperfections. He talked about owning an old Victorian-era house once upon a time and how he hated working on its corroded plumbing. The building I had quickly fallen in love with had obviously stirred up unpleasant, old-building memories for him.

I learned there are often two types of people: the pioneers and the settlers. I have concluded that we are one of each. When the pioneer in me said, "I have an idea," it did not always produce happy responses for my husband, who is more of a settler. Blending our personality types has required patience from both of us. Teamwork has often been challenging. When we found ways to work together, we functioned as a team, but those times were simply a gift.

While we were upstairs, he jumped up and down on the worn wood floor. Then he finally said, "You're right — this is a good, solid old building." I received his first positive comment as my green light to passionately respond with, "Yes, isn't it great? Can't you just see people dancing on these wood floors and how wonderful this place could be again?" At that moment, he was obviously not ready to wholeheartedly partake of my enthusiasm. I remember him saying something about not wanting to work on rotten plumbing, and I got quiet again.

He finally said he thought I had the administrative skills to take on such a big project. He believed I could manage it. He agreed that I could at least get more information about the building, but he reminded me that we had no money to put toward the effort. I would have to come up with the cash somehow. Perhaps he thought that, without money, he was safe in letting me look into the purchase (smile). In that moment, I had what was needed most: A vision and a passion for the building's restoration.

Dick gave me the name and phone number of the Grange Master. As Tim and I drove home, I felt pregnant with new possibilities. With Tim's somewhat reluctant, but courageous, consent, I called Don, the Grange Master, later that night. He and I had a short conversation. It went something like this: "Mr. Gammon, I sure do like your grange hall. I think it could continue to be a great community-meeting place. I see a lot of life left in your building. I would really like to restore it so that people could continue to gather there." He responded with, "Well, another square-dance group has offered me $10,000 for it." I quickly said, "Well, I will give you $11,000. But I would like to have it inspected and will need to talk to county officials about it first." To which he responded, "Well, OK then. I guess it's yours. Take all the time you need." Yes, it really was that easy to buy the old grange hall on a simple verbal agreement, no money down, and not even a handshake. I later learned that Dick had told Don that I was going to call. He said, "I think you should sell the building to Linda; I think she'll do something good with it."

Now, I should mention that I did not have the $11,000 when I boldly made my offer. I didn't have even $1,000. Well, I didn't tell Don I had the money. I said that I would give him $11,000. I am thankful I had two moms in my life that financially supported my vision: My mother, Mary Lou, and mother-in-law, Ludmila. They each lent me half of the $11,000 that I needed to purchase the building, and I did eventually pay them back. My "Other Mother," Glenda, cheered me on and prayed for me. There is nothing quite like having moms who are enthusiastic fans. That is the kind of mom I always wanted to be — one who would champion her children's dreams and encourage them.

And that is how I became the new owner of the 1911 Mountain View Grange #429/Lewisburg Hall & Warehouse Company — next to the railroad track, on the highway — that "nobody in her right mind would live in." I had a vision for the building's restoration but not much money. Although I never had the desire to take on such a project, the Lewisburg Hall restoration project was birthed. She was my new baby, and she needed a lot of love and nurturing.

> *...he is able to do exceedingly and abundantly*
> *beyond all you can ask or imagine...*
> *— Ephesians 3:20*

Meanwhile, I continued working as the Resource Development Director for the Boys and Girls Club. I organized fundraising events, promoted programs, helped build community relationships, and juggled multiple tasks simultaneously. For eight years, I also directed the 1857 Charles Gaylord House restoration. In addition, I used my modest paycheck and began a seven-year restoration of the Lewisburg Hall. I initially thought the project would take only a couple of years and would cost much less than it eventually did.

They say, "Ignorance is bliss." Had I known what would be required of me by the city, county, and state building officials, I might not have had the courage to take on such an enormous and expensive project. I say, "I might not have." Then again, I have not always made decisions using the logical side of my brain. Some decisions I simply made with my heart.

The restoration of historic buildings often takes longer and costs more than can be known in the beginning of a project. There is a term called "The Mushroom Factor," which recognizes that the scope of an historic preservation project usually mushrooms into more problems, more needs, and greater costs. "Scope Creep" happens. Once we preservationists have dived into a restoration project, however, problem situations do not usually discourage us. My mom always called me "tenacious" because I could devote myself to something I cared about and not quit. She admired that I was steadfast and passionate when I was involved in a mission. When it came to historical preservation work — and many other aspects of life — I found that having a steadfast determination was essential.

In those days, I wore many hats. I was busy directing fundraising events, leading restoration projects, and taking care of home responsibilities. While I made my "to do" lists, I assumed that, because I did not have children, I could take on more work than most women. Multitasking at an intense level energized me. The role of a "one-woman band" was how I enjoyed living life. Even though I loved what I was doing, however, I drew too much energy from my body's "happy juice." It was a particularly exhilarating season for me. My body's adrenaline fueled my passions. I often worked fourteen- to sixteen-hour days, but there was always more work that could be done. I sometimes did not know when to stop. I definitely needed to learn a healthy work-rest balance and how to set boundaries. I loved what I was doing and did not even consider reining myself in. I was like a horse running wild in a meadow on a windy day.

"I have found that dreams can be realized with a lot of passion,
steadfast faith, and a healthy dose of determination."
— Linda Dodson

My imagination was continuously sparked by creative ideas. I was so inspired and absorbed in my work that I sometimes even forgot to eat. My joy was my food. It was difficult to turn my mind and my adrenaline flow off at night so that I could sleep. I mistakenly thought that, if I loved what I was doing, it would not be stressful for my body. I was wrong. I learned that life and people would gladly take all I had to give. My body began to show signs of weakening. I was stressed because my calendar was too full, my "to do" lists were too long, and I was usually short on sleep. A few people close to me said I gave away too much of myself. I admit that, in those days, I did not schedule enough time for my own interests or for my personal restoration. Even after all the airplane flights I had taken, I had forgotten the important in-flight emergency procedure: "Put your own oxygen mask on first." I gave almost everyone and everything else priority in my life.

After years of being immersed in building projects, leading teams, and juggling many tasks, in 1997 I experienced a BIG crash landing. I'd spent hundreds of overtime hours directing a successful, major fundraising event. My body descended from its adrenaline high, and I hit rock bottom, hard. I dragged myself through the days and weeks that followed. My condition scared me. I had never felt so weak and exhausted. I accumulated enough overtime hours at my job that I could take a much-needed two-month paid leave of absence. I really had no choice but to take time away from my work. I was barely able to function.

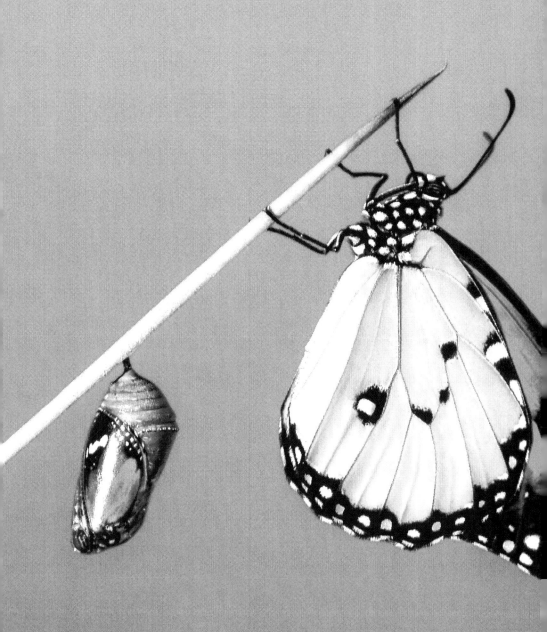

11.
PUSHING THE
"PAUSE" BUTTON

During my time off, I spent my days mostly lying in a quiet room, staring out the tall window at the end of my couch. Television was too stimulating to watch. My large Bible was too heavy to hold. I did not feel like talking on the phone. Most people were unaware of how sick I was. My happy-face mask was securely fastened. At that time, there was no Internet connection at my home and no Facebook, Instagram, Twitter, Kakao, or WeChat to communicate with people — those were disconnected times. I still miss getting a handwritten letter or card in my mailbox.

In 1997, when I hit the "pause" button on my big projects and the people I had worked with, my sense of purpose was also suspended. Looking back, I am thankful that I even stayed mentally sane during that isolated time of severe physical exhaustion. Many chronic-fatigue sufferers have battled suicidal thoughts. Thankfully, I never got to that low point of emotional despair.

Two months later, when I returned to work at the Corvallis Boys and Girls Club, I quickly realized that my creativity was not flowing. Compared to my former years of running on high energy and being a prolific producer, I did not have the inspired edge I needed to succeed at my job. One glance at my tired face in the mirror each morning was proof that I was burnt out. Once I weaned myself off of the adrenaline rush I had relied on, I realized I was barely running on fumes and needed an overhaul.

During our major fundraising event, the Corvallis community had learned about the mission and programs of our Boys and Girls Club. Our next big goal was to launch a capital campaign to raise funds for a new, multi-million-dollar youth facility for the children of our city. I looked forward to directing that campaign. When I could no longer do my best work, however, I knew I had to resign so that my replacement could be hired to lead the marketing and fundraising effort. It was stressful knowing I could not give the Club, the children, and their families the attention they deserved and feeling that I had abandoned the people I worked with. I always tried to give my work a 100-percent effort. OK — maybe even a 120-percent effort. Unfortunately, I was no longer operating at the top of my game.

When I resigned from my job and volunteer restoration projects, I grieved the loss of work I had loved. Without my monthly paycheck, I also knew I would not be able to continue with the restoration of the Lewisburg Hall, so that project also went inactive. The Hall needed a lot more restoration, but so did I.

I was forced to focus on recovering my health. For many months, I lay on the same couch. There were days when I actually crawled from my bed, down the hallway, to that couch. Where I was once a passionate and inspired leader, I felt almost no motivation or enthusiasm. Life felt flat. I was the product of a burnout of my own doing. I was guilty of not giving myself adequate rest, nutrition, and exercise, and of working too long and hard. Months later, Dan, a man I had worked with on projects, loved me enough to tell me how terrible I looked in those days. Faithful are the wounds of a friend.

As an introvert, I had neglected the unscheduled time I needed to recharge my own batteries. My energy level was about only twenty percent of what it had been. In my forties, what should have been my prime time, my vitality and passion had left. As a leader, I needed my contagious enthusiasm back. In the past, I had been able to inspire others, but I suddenly felt uninspiring. My primary-care doctor at the Corvallis Clinic eventually diagnosed me with Epstein Barr Virus (EBV) or chronic fatigue syndrome (CFS), although he said he did not know much about the disease. I was absolutely exhausted and felt almost no enthusiasm or creative inspiration.

At that time, most doctors commonly believed that EBV/CFS was "just in the head" of its sufferers. There were no definitive lab tests to confirm the illness. My primary care doctor did not really know how to help me, but, thankfully, he believed my chronic fatigue was real. He invited me to come see him anytime I needed to. I had appointments every couple of months. He listened to me, checked my vital signs, and ordered basic blood tests. The only medication he prescribed for me was sleeping pills, because, even though I was extremely fatigued, I had trouble sleeping.

Many years later, when I finally improved, Dr. Peter told me I had actually encouraged him. As an oncologist, he had lost many of his patients to cancer. I was one of his patients who, very gradually, improved. My friend, Rich, a nuclear physicist at California's Lawrence Livermore National Laboratory, also became interested in chronic fatigue due to my suffering. He studied my case, encouraged me, and made some important discoveries and contributions to CFS research before his death in 2012.

I managed to get to the market for groceries and to church most Sundays. I tried to spend time in nature, which helped. I had to be extremely careful while driving. My focus was terrible, and my brain was extremely foggy, which made me a danger on the road. I was not surprised to learn that the IQ of chronic-fatigue sufferers was actually lower during their illness. My mind was definitely dull. It was difficult to have all my projects cut off, taking with them my teams, my new identity, and the satisfaction I had knowing I was making positive contributions in my community.

While my husband was at work, I was held hostage at home by excessive fatigue. I had no children to keep me company or help me. I was free from tasks and demands, but I mourned the loss of human connection and the projects that had brought me joy. Thankfully, the womb of silence I lived in birthed something deeper and more meaningful in my life. As I considered my situation, I saw that, in my dark, set-apart place, I was not really alone. I was being carried.

Isolation invited me to let go of the busyness and former distractions of my life. I accepted my condition as a new opportunity to enter a place of restfulness. I allowed myself to be redefined — not by my work or my accomplishments but by gaining a deeper awareness of whose I was. I let go of my performance orientation and welcomed resting and just being. I wish I could say that I made the most of every day. The truth is that there were days when I felt unproductive and dull.

Day by day, my home became a sanctuary of peaceful contemplation and prayer. Better yet, my depleted physical condition allowed me to tune in to the inner voice of the spirit and become a better friend of God. Though He did not cause my illness, in my weakness and my time of holy isolation, He brought me close. Those were the days when my pain gave me the opportunity to lean on Him and not on other people.

"Our rest lies in looking to the Lord, not to ourselves."
— Watchman Nee

As I practiced stillness, I was strengthened. I was a developing chrysalis in the cocoon of His loving presence until my wings were ready to fly. As I surrendered to my limitations, I found peace and learned to flow prayerfully. That was my season of spiritual metamorphosis. I accepted the set-apart time as my opportunity to be spiritually deepened. I gained contentment in my identity as simply "His beloved daughter." I embraced Him in my struggle. My couch by the window was where I was strengthened and reborn as a woman of prayer and felt deeply loved by my Creator.

Song: "Perfect Peace," by Laura Story

Song: "You Say," by Lauren Daigle

Song: "You Raise Me Up," by Josh Groban

12.
KEEP ON
KEEPING ON

Weeks later, I still felt fatigued. In bed at night, my brain was still stuck in the "on" position, but my body desperately needed to be switched "off." As I battled sleeplessness, I considered the steps I could take to improve my health. Thankfully, I discovered a helpful book on chronic fatigue syndrome (CFS), and I started making positive changes: a healthier diet, rest, reduced stress, time in nature, prayer, and a calming of my mind. I began believing that my health could improve and that there were better days ahead. I chose to be a willing partner in my healing process. In the past, I had said "Yes" to the many requests of others. I finally said "Yes" to me.

My husband was busy with his career and his early-to-bed, early-to-rise routines. My goal each day was basic: shower, dress, and figure out something to have for dinner; sometimes we just ate the best soup I could buy and salad from a bag. At my weakest, I could not hold myself upright at the table for long. My body felt like lead, similar to the downward pull one feels while riding a Ferris wheel.

In addition to infertility, I suffered with chronic fatigue. I was among the millions of women who were infertile, but I did not have safe places to talk about my feelings. Even though I felt sad and depleted, I realized that everyone had challenges. And nobody really likes a whiner, right? Talking about how I felt was tiring, too personal, and, frankly, quite boring. I was never a fan of pulling people into my drama. It takes commitment to journey with people in pain. I confess that I'm not the best with this group. I decided to set others free from listening to the details of my struggles. That part of isolation was not my friend.

Somehow, my friend Gloria found out that I was health challenged. During my first Christmas with chronic fatigue, when my energy was at its lowest point, she and her daughters arranged to surprise me. They cleaned our house, decorated a small tree, and left us dinner. I experienced how heartwarming acts of kindness can be when people feel poorly. Their blessing showed me the power of caring for the hurting. I like to pass on their kind of love.

I am thankful that I never doubted the value of my life. When I was in survival mode and my physical recovery was at a snail's pace, I gained forty pounds. Unfortunately, it was not baby weight. I experienced hair loss, severe body weakness, and an inability to do strenuous work. I missed expressing myself through my work. As an infertile woman, another emotional milestone came when my menstruation ended. My body was so low on energy that it reached the end of its reproductive fertility. In those days of feeling like an old woman, I wondered if I would grow old before I got well or felt young again. It took me nearly ten years to fully regain my health and to begin thriving again. Eventually, my courage overcame my fears.

When my youthful get-up-and-go left, I experienced loss. I had identified myself as a community volunteer and I felt joy when I helped to preserve local history, but my sense of purpose also exited. My work had filled some of my motherhood void, but then, all of a sudden, my projects were eliminated, and my new identity hit a wall. Without my job, there was no income to continue restoring Lewisburg Hall. The restoration of historic buildings costs money, a truckload of cash. It pained me to put my restoration project on the back burner. I trusted that something good would happen to provide for its restoration. I had experienced a truth that is more than an embroidery slogan:

"When a vision is given, the provision comes."

When I first purchased the Lewisburg Hall, a reporter from the Corvallis Gazette Times (GT) called to ask if she could interview me about my project. She wanted the scoop on the woman who was restoring the historic grange hall. Since chronic fatigue had settled in around my vision, I was not sure if I wanted my story told. I thought I might feel too pressured, knowing that people in my community were watching and expected to see progress. The building was highly visible, since it was located beside Oregon Highway 99W. When the reporter said that the newspaper photographer had already captured a photograph with a rainbow arching over my building, I thought it was a positive sign and decided to give her the interview. Her wonderful story, along with the rainbow photo, was featured on the front page of the GT. Its hopeful symbolism was an encouragement to me.

When could I resume the restoration of "The Hall"? Its future was uncertain. My big, rundown baby awaited her much-needed love and attention, but she had to wait — and so did I.

For the revelation awaits an appointed time;
it speaks of the end and will not prove false.
Though it linger, wait for it;
it will certainly come and will not delay.
— Habakkuk 2:3

13.
WITH VISION
COMES PROVISION

In 1985, prior to my chronic-fatigue diagnosis, I joined with 200,000 other women and men in a class-action lawsuit with the A. H. Robins Company, the manufacturer of the Dalkon Shield intrauterine device (IUD) I had used for birth control. Women who used the presumed-safe IUD had reported physical injury, miscarriage, pelvic inflammatory disease, and permanent infertility. Some husbands also filed claims due to the tragic death of their wives.

After responding to a notice in the New York Times about the lawsuit in 1986, I received a fifty-page questionnaire to fill out. In the forms, the question was asked, "How has not being able to have children affected your life?" There was so much I could say in response. I relived memories as I wrote and sometimes cried. I was thankful to learn that I was not required to have an attorney, and I chose to represent myself. For me, it was a cost-saving decision. About seventy-one percent of the claimants represented themselves. The Trust handled 218,000 claims and worked hard to maintain equal treatment of those with or without legal representation. They did not want to give an unfair advantage to claimants who could afford to hire attorneys. I appreciated the simplicity of completing the forms, attaching my medical records, and being done with the process.

There were three claim options to choose from. I was among the "Option 3 claimants": 47,000 women who had suffered the most severe physical injuries, including permanent infertility. I filed my claim, as a matter of principle, and did not expect to receive much compensation, if any. How could I even put a monetary value on my ability, or inability, to have a baby and raise my child?

From 1974 to 1985, the legal process was discussed in the courts as the Trust reorganized and refined their plan. In 1989 litigation work began on the Option 3 claims, a process that took more than one year and was finalized in 2000. I would occasionally receive a newsletter updating me on the status of the Dalkon Shield Claimants' Trust. From my observation, they did their best to handle the claims honorably and cost efficiently. In the end, the Trust charged only a modest $400 administration fee to process each claim.

During the first December of my chronic fatigue in 1989, I was resigned from my job. I spent most of my time resting, but I was still feeling exhausted. Since I had no income to finance the enormous, expensive project, I wondered how I would ever restore my Lewisburg Hall. Just before Christmas, I received a notice saying that there was a classified letter waiting for me at the post office. The sender was "Dalkon Shield Claimants' Trust, Richmond, VA." I figured it was another newsletter updating me on the Trust's progress. However, when I opened the envelope at the post office, there was a letter addressed directly to me asking if I would accept their settlement offer.

After almost seven years of my claim pending, an offer came, and I accepted it. I referred to the settlement as "my baby money." My check arrived at Christmas, an appropriate holiday for an unexpected arrival. Provision came at the perfect time. The settlement enabled me to resume the restoration of the Lewisburg Hall. A gentle, refreshing breeze began to gently blow over my life again. My preservation project was happily reignited.

> *...but those who hope in the LORD*
> *will renew their strength.*
> *They will soar on wings like eagles.*
> *They will run and not grow weary.*
> *They will walk and not be faint.*
> *— Isaiah 40:31*

My health was definitely not its best when I pushed the restart button on my project. I was functioning at about fifteen percent of my former energy. One day, when I tried to sand a wooden chair, I became so exhausted after only ten minutes that I had to stop. I decided to focus instead on the less strenuous task of nominating Lewisburg Hall to the National Register of Historic Places. I thought I could probably manage to research, read newspaper articles on the library's microfilm, and write. It would be an honor if I could get my building listed on the esteemed National Register.

With the help of my friend Mary and other preservation specialists at the Oregon State Historic Preservation Office (SHPO), I conducted interviews and researched its history. My friend, Lynn, took black-and-white pictures for the photographic documentation. In 1991, we celebrated as the Lewisburg Hall and Warehouse Company/ Mountain View Grange #429 was nominated and accepted to the National Register of Historic Places in Washington, DC. The 1857

Charles Gaylord House I had helped rescue from demolition was also added to the National Register that day.

I was thankful that two significant historical structures that were entrusted to my care were honored at the national level. As a steward of those historic buildings, I was able to make a lasting contribution to local history and leave a legacy that is still meaningful to me.

I have always loved envisioning, designing, planning, and fulfilling dreams. Remember, my motto was: "You gotta love it!" Even in my depleted condition, I could enjoy these activities as I planned for the Lewisburg Hall's future restoration. My first major task was to create a preservation plan. Eventually a team of people came to help me realize my plan. Each month, my health improved a tiny bit. The heaviness I had carried in my body was gradually replaced by a lighter, brighter version of me.

My dad once said that he thought the joy I experienced during the restoration of Lewisburg Hall contributed to my own physical recovery. Dad was right. The restoration of the Lewisburg Hall was an amazing seven-year project. I was thankful for all the people who helped me fulfill my vision. Thanks, Tim, for supporting my restoration of the Lewisburg Hall and for believing I could do it.

14.
TEAMWORK

The restoration of Lewisburg Hall began with a vision. The front-page newspaper article, with its photograph of the rainbow arching over my building, did attract public attention. As I had expected, interested people would occasionally stop by to see how the restoration was progressing. In the project's early phase, demolition work came first. We uncovered original features hidden beneath the more recent top layers. As we removed non-historic materials, we could uncover the building's problems that lay underneath and needed to be worked on.

> *"Teamwork makes the dream work!"*
> — *John Maxwell*

It was a joy to begin restoring "my baby" again. During demolition, we removed fluorescent light fixtures, plywood and acoustic panels covering tongue-and-groove walls, and tiles glued onto Douglas fir ceilings and floors. Uncovering the building's original features was like a treasure hunt. One day I pulled back some light-green plywood and made the fun discovery of original, unpainted tongue-

and-groove wood walls underneath. We removed an outdated wood-burning stove, an oil-burning furnace, old bathroom fixtures, and 1950s appliances. We cut out rotten wood and galvanized pipes. Yes, my husband, Tim, did help remove the old, corroded plumbing. Bless his heart.

We replaced unsafe wiring, iron-stained porcelain fixtures, kitchen sinks, and the steep entry ramp not built to modern American With Disabilities Act (ADA) codes. We brought in five-panel doors, fir cabinets, metal light shades, coffee cans filled with butterfly hinges, and a claw-foot bathtub. I scored thirty turn-of-the-century Douglas fir benches that were the right architectural style for seating. We salvaged old building materials from other historic buildings that were slated for demolition. Many of the vintage parts and valuable items I had collected were stored inside the building until they could be used.

The building's interior was quite a sight — a big mess in the eyes of most people. It was a huge task to continually move parts around as we worked on each area of the building. In the beginning of the restoration, I invited the former Grange members to have lunch at the Lewisburg Hall while they were still able. They were gracious when they saw that I had removed some of the features they had added to "modernize" the spaces. Most of them understood that the goal of a building on the Historic Register was to restore its features to the original design. They mostly seemed relieved and happy that their old grange hall was going to live on.

In this world, there are "WOW people" and "WHY people."
Which group are you in?

To most people, it looked like my project was going backward instead of forward, getting worse instead of better. When people came by to take a look, I could see that my project attracted two kinds of people: (1) the "Wow people" and (2) the "Why people." From my observation, I learned that only a small percentage of them were "Wow people," who could see what my building was becoming. When they walked into the messy "work in progress," they usually said, "Wow, this is beautiful!" They did not seem bothered at all by the temporary disorder.

The second group were the "Why people." They walked in slowly and cautiously with a deer-in-the-headlights look on their faces, sometimes shaking their heads "No." They did not make positive comments, and they usually had concerned looks on their faces. I smiled inside when I saw the "Why people." I knew they just could not see past the mess and the building's promising future. In their eyes, I think they saw me as a misguided, crazy woman. A few "Why people" were members of my own family. Those who love us are often protective, which is not always a bad thing. When my stepfather first toured "The Hall" in its early phase, he kept whispering, "Sell, sell." He later applauded my accomplishments when he could finally see what the building had become.

As I worked to bring my vision to fruition, I was thankful for all the "Wow people" on my team. It takes only a few enthusiastic friends to add fuel to the fire of one's passion. I was grateful I could envision the possibilities. Being able to see the potential in something or in someone is a requirement for a restoration specialist and for one who is a lover and supporter of people.

Life is full of amazing possibilities. Let's dream on!

One day, when I was at the Hall working, Pastor Linda came to visit me. As we sat upstairs, she told me about a vision she had when she was traveling. She looked out her airplane window and saw how people had changed the landscape of planet Earth with their tilling and planting. That is when the Lord told her that my life would change the spiritual landscape of Earth with many beautiful and productive fertile fields, for His glory. Oh, that is not how I always felt. Too many times, I had allowed my identity to be diminished by my reproductive infertility and childlessness. I was encouraged to hear her vision of God's perspective on my life.

My restoration team was dynamite, the best I could have hoped for. Many gave generously, and some even volunteered their time because they wanted to be part of the historic event. I appreciated every contributor. Others donated old house parts, Douglas fir lumber, and their talents. They refinished cabinets, sewed beautiful curtains, and planted flowers. My neighbor occasionally mowed the lawn and trapped gophers. My young niece organized little parts in small see-through bags. Others cleaned, encouraged, and advised. I appreciated every act of kindness and loved working with a unified team toward a common goal. Spending my days with other "Wow people" was the wind beneath my wings.

With the help of many talented contractors and a dedicated team of friends and family, the seven-year restoration of the 1911 Lewisburg Hall & Warehouse Company/Mountain View Grange #429 was completed just in time for my church friends, Sean and Leiah's December wedding reception. What an amazing journey it was, an undertaking beyond anything I had ever imagined. One of my first helpers was Steve, who repaired all the cotton sash ropes in the large double-hung windows. When he came to visit six years later, he kept saying, "You did it — you really did it. It's just like you said it would be!" Many people celebrated with me when the restoration was completed.

Lewisburg Hall has continued to be a memorable place for people to gather. We restored her, and they came. With the help of my great staff, we hosted thousands of guests. Over a seven-year period, there were about eight hundred events, such as weddings, receptions, rehearsal dinners, reunions, birthdays, meetings, parties, quilt-ins, dances, hymn sings, and concerts. Hewlett-Packard even held top-secret meetings they called "The Grange Project." It was a blessing to use my "baby money" to restore her and have fruitful purpose birthed in my life.

It was challenging to lovingly restore my building and then open her doors to the public. When people came, they sometimes caused damage. Despite our "no-high-heels-please" policy and the flat shoes we provided at the front entrance, a lady wore her spiked high heels with their protective pads worn off. Everywhere she walked, the nails on her high heels punched permanent holes in the newly refinished, historic wood floors. Oh, my!

I learned how important it was to save and restore the historic buildings in our communities. Preserving them strengthened the foundations of us all. People expressed their appreciation for the restoration of the Lewisburg Hall. It was lovingly saved and renovated by the people and for the people. I was humbled to receive two awards: (1) A "Certificate of Recognition — for giving the community outstanding service in historical preservation" from the Winema Chapter of the Daughters of the American Revolution on February 15, 1996, and (2) "The Cultural Resources Preservation Award for Outstanding Contributions in Preserving Benton County's Historical and Cultural Heritage," for Tim and Linda Dodson, from the Benton County Historical Resources Commission on May 1,

1996. I felt privileged to simply be a caretaker of a special historic place, for my appointed time in history.

As "proprietor," I hosted family celebrations, many came for baby showers, weddings, bar and bat mitzvahs, birthday parties, and reunions. During those intergenerational events, my mother's heart would sometimes reawaken from its place of hibernation. I was caught off guard at the reactions I felt when I saw little girls in party dresses, and attentive, loving moms with their bride daughters at weddings. As I witnessed the memorable life events of others, I was reminded again that I would never be able to experience the same tender moments with my own son or daughter. Through the years, there were times when I let myself experience the feelings that my childlessness caused. At other times, I suppressed my emotions when I feared they might overwhelm me. I wondered when, or if, I would ever be free of my loss and the pain of infertility.

I discovered that the matter of legacy was an important one for me. At the end of my life, I wanted to have no regrets, to have fully realized my purpose, and to leave behind a legacy of love. I was thankful I could help preserve some historic places that would hopefully live well into the future. I recently got a text message from Miranda. She and her husband were married at the Hall almost two decades ago. They requested a photograph of Lewisburg Hall for their living room wall. It was heartwarming to know that my special place was still their happy place.

Though I cannot leave the legacy of children on my branch of the family tree, I made a contribution when I poured my heart and my "baby money" into the restoration of a significant historical place. By preserving the Lewisburg Hall, I left a legacy.

SCENE 4:
UNEXPECTED
BLESSINGS

If you lay down the life you have always wanted,
you just might find you will receive something better.

15.
A DIVINE INTERRUPTION AND
SPIRITUAL SABBATICAL

Ever since I was a young girl, I have loved surprises. In 1999, something unexpected happened when my husband and I attended a church-board retreat on the Oregon coast. At that gathering, Pastor Tom shared a video with board members and their spouses of a spiritual revival that was taking place at the Brownsville Assembly of God Church in Pensacola, Florida. The video showed their choir worshipping enthusiastically. As I watched, I thought, That is a place of unrestrained joy. I want to go there!

A seed was planted in my heart that day for a divine interruption in our life. Our friends John and Lisa were living in Florida, where the revival was taking place. John was enlisted in U.S. Naval flight training in Pensacola. So, we decided to take a trip to Florida to see them and visit the Brownsville revival they were also a part of.

On our first night at the Brownsville Assembly of God Church, I felt such an awe and reverence as we entered the building. I had been to different churches before, but I had never encountered a presence as strong as I did that night. The atmosphere in the sanctuary felt thick with peace. The woman sitting next to me said she smelled the aroma of freshly baked bread. Another lady said she smelled fragrant roses. As I sat down in the sanctuary, I felt like a blanket of warm love wrapped itself around me.

At the nightly services, we witnessed people being healed from all kinds of emotional and physical conditions. Some people received their healing just sitting in His presence. At the Friday night baptism service, men, women, and children told stories of being set free from their addictions and sorrows. Prostitutes told about feeling a love and acceptance they had never known before. The church applauded and cheered as each one shared their testimony. I was amazed by the healings I saw with my own eyes. It was obvious that miracles were still available.

As we drew close, He brought freedom. There was an atmosphere of holiness and permission to worship wholeheartedly with singing, dancing, and hands raised upward. People of all ages knelt, wept, and were even unable to stay standing. Some fell to the floor and sometimes remained there for a while. Blanket ladies would cover those who were resting in the spirit to protect their modesty and personal experience. It was truly a life-changing place for many people. As unusual as it all seemed, I felt at peace in the middle of the supernatural events. The Bible confirmed what I was witnessing:

...and the priests could not perform their service because of the cloud,
for the glory of the Lord filled the temple of God.
— 2 Chronicles 5:14

A favorite evening for me was the Tuesday-night prayer service. Hundreds of people gathered in groups around a dozen or more beautiful handmade banners to focus their prayers on subjects such as family, the nations, healing, souls, pastors, schools, children, and the peace of Jerusalem. Musicians played inspirational music as we prayed and worshipped. I felt drawn to the "Revival in America" banner. As I knelt there, I began to feel deep grief for my nation, the United States of America. I had never experienced such an intense sorrow during prayer as I did that night. I eventually lay on the carpet and wept for my country for quite a while. A deep desire to see a spiritual awakening was birthed in me that night. To this day, I carry that desire for America and for several other nations in the world.

"Let us recognize this one thing: burden is the secret of prayer.
If a person does not feel within him a burden to pray for a
particular matter, he can hardly succeed in prayer. In a prayer
meeting, some brothers and sisters may mention a great many
subjects for prayer. If you are not touched inwardly, you cannot pray."
— Watchman Nee, Christian Teacher

The Brownsville Assembly of God Church was known for being a church of integrity, where holiness was preached, prayer was central, and having a heart for the nations was utmost. Led by Pastor John Kilpatrick, a two-year prayer initiative for revival began in 1993. Two years of prayer by the church members culminated in what is now known as the "Pensacola Outpouring" or the "Brownsville Revival."

The Brownsville Revival began in 1995, during a Sunday morning Father's Day service. While visiting Evangelist Steve Hill was preaching, the Spirit began moving, and people's hearts were touched. Pastor John Kilpatrick, a well-respected leader and Senior Pastor, was so overcome by the Spirit that he fell to the floor and remained there for most of the service. Pastor Kilpatrick was always dressed handsomely, like a model in the fashionable Gentleman's

Quarterly magazine. He was a most unlikely man to lie on the carpeted stage in his perfectly pressed shirt and suit. As Steve Hill preached his message, many people experienced God's loving touch. History records that Father's Day marked a new beginning for the Brownsville Assembly of God Church and for its faithful people.

For the next seven years, more than seven million people who were hungry for God visited that revival from all over the world. They waited in long lines for hours just to get into the church, sometimes camping in tents as they waited. Brownsville hosted the longest revival in American history and was marked by notable physical, emotional, and spiritual healings — and by the presence of God. I witnessed the awesomeness of God and felt grateful and humbled to be part of the historic outpouring.

What I experienced at the Brownsville Revival was a game-changer in my life. After returning to Oregon, I continued to pursue a deeper friendship with God. I kept hearing the phrase "Led by His Spirit (LBHS)." As a reminder, I wrote "LBHS" on little sticky notes and posted them around my house and in my car. Being "Led by His Spirit" became a life focus and an important key to unlocking doors in my life.

In my quiet time back home, I had an increasing desire to return to Pensacola, Florida, to attend the Brownsville Revival School of Ministry. After two weeks of praying about it, I got the courage to tell my husband what I was feeling. It was certainly unexpected timing to consider a cross-country move, because we had just settled into the "dream house" we'd finished building the year before. I had the great joy of designing our two-story, 1890s-style farmhouse and overseeing the details of its construction. Our home was a peaceful place and the fulfillment of a long-awaited personal dream. As I spent many hours with large sheets of paper, sharpened Ticonderoga #2 pencils, and T-squares drawing house plans, I never imagined that I would soon consider giving up the dream house we had waited fourteen years to build. I could not deny, however, the invitation that I felt being extended to us.

At that time, I met weekly with four prayer buddies: Becky, Carole, Pastor Linda, and Sandy. They prayed for me as we considered leaving it all to go to Florida. Tim also talked to Pastor Tom about the idea of us attending BRSM. Tom told Tim that he should seriously consider saying, "Yes" if he thought we were being called to go. "God doesn't always knock twice," he added. In the weeks and months that followed, much prayer and fasting went into our big decision.

Understandably, some of our family members were uncomfortable with the idea. It was certainly not "normal," or "logical" to give up a new home, leave stable jobs and financial security, and move across the country toward an uncertain future. Tim's son and family had also just moved from New York to Oregon. They were not happy with the idea of us leaving them. Were we going to be pastors, missionaries, or worship leaders? We did not know. Some said if we were not sure why we were going, it was probably not a good idea or a God idea. Others had heard about the unusual things happening at the revival and were skeptical, even openly critical.

We did not have an end goal in mind beyond just trusting and saying, "Yes" to the invitation. My Father was concerned that maybe we were joining a cult. Our generation was acquainted with cults like the one at Peoples' Temple at Jonestown in Guyana, South America, led by Jim Jones, which ended tragically in 1978. Jones reportedly led more than nine hundred of his followers in a mass suicide by drinking a cyanide-laced drink. When we saw that people were uncomfortable with our idea, we continued to pray and seek direction.

*"Prayer is more than a practice or a ritual. Prayer is powerful.
It brings the miraculous and connects us to our Maker. Adversity
offers us a wonderful opportunity to see the workings of an amazing,
caring God who is alive and who answers prayers on our behalf."*
— Linda Dodson

As our faith was stretched, I felt thankful for the friends and family members who observed our process and prayed for us. It was good to be surrounded by people who knew us well. They trusted that this radical idea could actually mean that something amazingly good was happening in our lives. As they listened and watched, I sensed some of them were also considering making changes in their lives.

One Sunday morning, my friend Lori led worship at our church. She sang one of my favorite hymns, "I'd Rather Have Jesus." Her lovely voice and lyrics so beautifully expressed the current feelings in my own heart: "I'd rather have Jesus than silver or gold. I'd rather be his than have riches untold. I'd rather have Jesus than houses or lands. I'd rather be led by his nail-pierced hands…I'd rather have Jesus than anything this world affords today." I went to the altar that morning and knelt to pray. Warm tears streamed down my face as her lovely voice serenaded me. As I surrendered my life, no doubts clouded my heart.

In the weeks and months that followed, a peaceful enthusiasm grew in my spirit. Tim continued to pray and seek wisdom about his decision. Like me, he is a firstborn child, a responsible one who has always taken his provider role seriously. Even though he had not reached a final decision, he supported me whittling down our possessions and packing boxes. He always did like having less "stuff."

Friends helped me take truckloads of donations to charity, usually when Tim was on a fishing trip, so he did not have to deal with the chaos at home. I felt directed to give items to certain people, which I enjoyed doing. I gave my friend Holly my large copper pot to hold her firewood and was led to tell her that she would be "a vessel for noble purposes," and she has been. It was a time in my life when I was tested on the matter of material possessions. One week, I filled my dining room table with valuables like crystal candleholders, linen napkins, silk tablecloths, a wool suit, and many other treasures. When my buddies came for prayer, I invited them to take whatever they wanted. It felt like early Christmas that fall day: cream-colored linen napkins for Becky, my burgundy Pendleton wool suit (that I bought with proceeds from the sale of my first magazine article) for Linda, and new tablecloths for Carole. In the process of downsizing, I learned that I enjoyed owning nice things, but they did not own me. It was a freeing realization.

One December day in 1999 during his quiet time, Tim read his Oswald Chambers devotional, "My Utmost for His Highest." In the daily message, Chambers talked about the times in a man's life when he would come to a fork in the road. He could choose the path of least resistance, perhaps the more comfortable direction, or he could choose the path of his utmost for God's highest. Tim said the text spoke right to his current decision. He knew he needed to choose the higher path and not stay in his comfort zone. He said, "Yes" that day to his invitation to go to Pensacola, Florida.

We filled out our applications for the Brownsville Revival School of Ministry (BRSM) and mailed them off. While we waited for a response, I continued to prepare for a possible cross-country move. A few months later, we received our acceptance letters from the school. In May, we listed our one-year-old dream house with a realtor, and a "For Sale" sign went up on our front lawn. We surrendered it all.

Two months later, our dream house had still not sold. Only one couple came to even look at it. Tim told his manager at the Oregon Department of Transportation (ODOT) that if we could find a renter for our house, he was planning to resign and go to BRSM in Florida. Two days later, a man responded to our newspaper ad. He was moving to our area for a new job at Oregon State University and needed to find a nice house for his family to rent.

The day Rick came to see our house, our neighbors were having their big, extravagant Fourth of July party. We took him to the party, where he enjoyed meeting our neighbors. The timing seemed to me like a divine set-up. When we returned to our house afterwards, we told him about our plans to go to the school of ministry in Florida if we could find the right renter. Rick said he felt like he was the answer to our prayers and that he just had to rent our house. He also knew that his wife and young son would love living in our new country home.

Since our mortgage and property taxes were covered by the rent payment, Tim submitted his resignation letter to ODOT. He later told me that he had to accept that God was ultimately our provider, and not himself. Like many people do, he always preferred routine and security. It was no small thing for Tim, "The Settler," to leave his comfort zone and head toward uncharted territory. I was proud of him.

I was thankful for both the supporters and the skeptics in our life. Both groups of people listened to us and observed our process. Their questions caused us to continue praying, to seek wisdom, and to consider the cost of our decision. In the end, our supportive friends rallied around us. Kyle and Holly hosted a lovely dinner party and invited our friends, who celebrated and prayed with us as we prepared to go.

By faith Abraham, when called to go to a place
he would later receive as his inheritance,
obeyed and went, even though he did
not know where he was going.
— Hebrews 11:8

I tried to sell the Lewisburg Hall before we left, but I received no offers. We would understand later why our building did not sell. We bought a used Nissan "Quest" van that could tow a small trailer and took enough belongings to make our Florida apartment feel a little like home. My capable staff agreed to manage Lewisburg Hall in my absence, and we left Oregon in July of 2000. Most of our possessions were moved to storage or were loaned to friends. The preparation required extensive "stuff management." I felt both peace and a joyful anticipation that strengthened me for the task.

The night before we left town, we had dinner at Rex and Carole's house with my prayer buddies and husbands. Those special friends had faithfully prayed for us during our nine-month process. Our new opportunity was carried full term before it was birthed. As we drove up the I-5 freeway the next day on our new adventure, I called several friends to share the moment. We felt joyful and expectant.

You will go out with joy and be led forth with peace.
— Isaiah 55:12

We arrived in Pensacola, Florida, just in time to celebrate with John and Lisa as he received his U.S. Navy wings. We found an apartment in a lovely complex near our friends and got a few basic items to furnish our new place. Our friends gave us their bed, and we bought a folding table and chairs for dining. We used a borrowed twin bed for a couch and camping chairs and a small, round table for living-room furniture. We unpacked some basic kitchen items and hung our clothes in the closet. I hung pictures from our Oregon home on the walls and put our "welcome" mat by the front door. It was not our two-story dream house, but our home away from home was adequate. Life was simple, and we were fine with that.

We traded our view of Oregon's meadows and evergreen trees for Florida's palm trees, sunsets, and thunderstorms out our apartment windows. Our two-bedroom unit on the third floor would be "home" for a while — for how long, we did not know. After nine months of processing our decision and receiving confirmation, we trusted we were in the right place at the right time.

Without faith, it's impossible to please God,
because anyone who comes to him
must believe that he exists and that
he rewards those who earnestly seek him.
— Hebrews 11:6

A few days after we arrived, we went to the Brownsville Revival School of Ministry and were warmly greeted by staff and student volunteers. At the registration table, we met Ben, a fifty-year-old dentist who'd left his dental practice to attend the school. He looked up at Tim and said, "I want to honor you for what you left to get here." It was a special man-to-man moment that we both appreciated.

The mood of the school was upbeat. There were 1,200 students, aged eighteen to eighty years. Everyone had a story to tell about how their lives had been interrupted and they'd come there. People left houses and lands, businesses and careers, family and friends, countries and cultures, to pursue a deeper spiritual life. We heard about the many sacrifices students had made and how their faith had been tested. A sacrifice was always required.

Sudip's Story

Our friend Sudip was in India in 1998, when he saw a Brownsville Revival School of Ministry (BRSM) brochure. In the brochure, there was a photograph showing people raising their hands as they worshipped. The picture sparked a desire in Sudip to go where people could worship freely. In Nepal, they could not make a lot of noise or worship enthusiastically. Churches were illegal until 1990. Christians still had to be cautious after that because there was no religious freedom. Until 1998, they worshipped primarily in homes, but they had to be careful. Even though the door to religious freedom had been opened slightly, churches in Nepal still faced persecution.

Nepal was the only Hindu kingdom in the world until 2005. Sudip wanted to be free to worship God, because he lived where the Christian faith was illegal and the government spied on their people. Converting someone to Christianity was punishable by one year in prison, and the sentence for baptizing someone was three years in prison. Things have still not changed much. Nepal is declared secular, and there are many Christians in prison. Churches are burned. Hindu fanatics threaten believers. It is still a big risk to be a believer in Nepal.

In 2000, Sudip finally got his opportunity to attend BRSM. He arrived from Nepal with one suitcase and speaking only a little English. The cab driver brought him to the school on a Sunday night at 11:00 p.m., but the school was closed. So, the driver brought him to his house to spend the night. His daughter was sick, so Sudip prayed for her. The next morning, the girl was healed! The father gave Sudip $40 and drove him to the school.

* * *

We heard many great testimonies of how people had learned about BRSM before coming there. There was an instant camaraderie among the students who had all made major life changes, in exchange for a deeper relationship with God and, possibly, an entirely new direction for their life. Students came to BRSM from twenty-two different nations. We all agreed that we felt fortunate to have time to focus on just our spiritual lives. When we allowed ourselves to be interrupted, we received a rich sabbatical.

Early-morning prayer at school was also a favorite time for me. I loved joining with others who loved to pray, especially those in the younger generation, who were full of sincere spiritual fire. The countless hours we spent in corporate worship were awesome, reverent, deeply personal, healing, and joyful. Inspired, life-giving Biblical messages were preached by pastors and teachers led by the spirit. They provided encouraging teaching and presented us with opportunities to grow. I appreciated seeing men and women go to the podium to preach. They often pulled out their prepared sermons but then folded and put them away and allowed the spirit to speak a different message through them. There was an attitude of reverence and a yielding to the spirit's leading.

I was transplanted into rich, fertile soil. We were all passionate for God. His presence seemed to increase in response to our hunger for more of Him. Trusting in His unchanging love helped us to lay down our own desires and welcome His plans.

> *Many are the plans in a person's heart,*
> *but it is the LORD's purpose that prevails.*
> *Proverbs 19:21*

Over a seven-year period, from 1995 to 2002, hundreds of thousands of lives were touched at the Brownsville Revival. In turn, those adoring people carried the love of God and the fire of revival to many nations. I have no doubt that the ripple effect of the Brownsville Revival is still changing lives and impacting nations. An emerging evangelist of this time, Daniel Kolenda, was one of our classmates. He has preached with Christ for all Nations to millions of people in Africa and around the world and recently spoke to the Adedotun Aremu Gbadebo III, His majesty the King of Abeokuta, Nigeria.

Words are inadequate to fully describe the experiences we had at the Brownsville Revival. I am thankful to have been there to draw close to His heart and to let my life and destiny be directed.

Invitation to a Women's Retreat

Just prior to our one-year anniversary at BRSM, my friend Pastor Linda invited me to California to pray for her women's retreat. I was eager to share with others the deep love I had received. I used some of our remaining few hundred dollars on a plane ticket and flew to the West Coast for a long weekend.

On the first day of the retreat, there was a teaching, followed by a time of prayer for the women. One of my favorite things to do was to gather with women to pray for one another. While praying for Monique, a young woman I had not met before, I envisioned babies, many babies. I privately prayed about why I saw so many babies. Was my vision symbolic, representing the birth of something new in her life, or was it literal? I had been taught to "be careful about predicting mates, dates, and babies." As an infertile woman, I had received prayer many times. People even prophesied my future baby. Some were certain I would become a mother. "It is just a matter of the right timing," they assured me, or "Things happen for a reason," they would say.

> *"The hardest thing about 'Everything happens for a reason'*
> *was waiting for the reason to come along."*
> *—Unknown*

When my baby did not come, I had the added burden of reconciling myself with the unfulfilled "promises" I had received. I knew the Bible said, "Ask and it will be given to you." (Matthew 7:7) I had asked for a baby many times, and others had asked for me, too. When I wrestled with the dreaded "Why?" question, the only answer my heart received was "Just trust."

I knew nothing about Monique's life, but the vision I saw with lots of babies seemed so clear. I decided not to speak about what I saw during our prayer time. The matter seemed too sensitive and personal. Instead, I told Pastor Linda later what I had seen. She explained that Monique really wanted to have a child. When I learned more about her, I was glad I had not said anything to her about the babies I envisioned. Pastor Linda strongly encouraged me, however, to have a private time with Monique to tell her what I saw. Although I felt hesitant, I trusted Linda's discernment and made time for my conversation with the young woman.

I felt cautious, humbled, and vulnerable as I briefly shared my infertility story with Monique. She saw that I could definitely relate to her inability to get pregnant. Unfortunately, I did not have a miraculous baby testimony to really encourage her. When I told her that, when we prayed for her, I saw lots of babies, Monique got very excited and seemed encouraged. That moment reminded me of the time my pastor handed me the diaper pin and told me I was going to have a baby soon. I had also experienced the hopeful feelings and excitement that came when other people were sure I would eventually get pregnant.

Oh, how I prayed I had done the right thing in sharing my vision. I felt uneasy because I did not want to be guilty of giving Monique any false hope. I knew what it felt like to be expectant and later disappointed — that was a common theme in my infertility journey. So, I prayed for His best plans to be revealed and for Monique to stay at rest and trust in His faithfulness to her. I never thought I should declare "Babies, babies, babies" to her, even though I saw them so vividly. Because of my own unanswered prayers, I could not say for sure that Monique would get pregnant. I wished I could, but I did not dare.

"Our prayers may be awkward.
Our attempts may be feeble.
But since the power of prayer is in the One
who hears it and not in the one who says it,
our prayers do make a difference."
— Max Lucado

Our conversation ended with Monique feeling expectant, and me feeling vulnerable and uncertain what the outcome would be for her and her husband. It is still interesting to me that God would give her a hopeful prophetic word through me, an infertile woman. Perhaps the vision applied some glue to the seams of her faith. You can imagine how happy and relieved I was to later learn that the year after I talked with and prayed for Monique, she delivered triplets! Wow!

After our first year at the school of ministry, our Oregon house and business had still not sold. Our bank-account balance got down to its last few hundred dollars, and we had no peace about using credit cards to stay at BRSM. We knew other students who had done that, but we always agreed to stay debt free. If it wasn't debt free, it wasn't for me. Some of our classmates wanted to become missionaries, pastors, or worship leaders. But after graduation, they had to find jobs doing whatever they could to pay off their big credit-card debts. For some, their debt delayed their ability to begin a new life. We agreed that using the credit card to stay at school would be our attempt to provide for ourselves. We continued to seek debt-free direction for our future.

Tim applied for engineering jobs in Florida. Though he was well qualified, he received no offers. At the end of our first year, we used our remaining cash to return to Oregon. We did not know if we would be able to sell our house or my business during the summer and possibly return for a second year at BRSM. So, we sold some things and gave other items away. After our amazing one-year sabbatical, we packed another trailer and planned to return to Oregon. Our renters were living in our dream house, but we could live in Lewisburg Hall temporarily; it was good that she had not sold.

As we drove away from Pensacola, Florida, I was grateful for all I had seen and experienced. God had become so close to my heart and so big in my eyes. I wanted to continue experiencing His greatness and remain confident in what He could do for me and through me.

I did not see all the details of my future, but I had grown closer to Him, and that was more than enough. I had laid down my worldly possessions and the life that I knew. I trusted that He had good plans. While we were there, I released any unfulfilled baby desires I still had and welcomed Him birthing new life in me.

> *…being confident of this, that he who began a good work in you*
> *will carry it on to completion until the day of Christ Jesus.*
> *— Philippians 1:6*

When we returned to Oregon, we lived in Lewisburg Hall — "next to the railroad tracks, on the highway, in the building that nobody in their right mind would live in" (smile). There were just enough events scheduled to cover my business expenses. Tim applied for a job at the Oregon Department of Transportation (ODOT), and within seven weeks he was hired. When he started his job at ODOT, he was considered a "rehire" since he had been gone less than two years. He got back the six hundred hours of sick leave and the forty hours of vacation time he had accrued before he'd resigned and left for Florida — a nice blessing.

Feeling confident that the doors had opened for us in Oregon, we notified our renters that we wanted to reoccupy our home. Four months later, we moved back into our house. It was a blessing to build a dream house once, but to get it back was like getting a dream house twice. When I gave up my most treasured possession, the house I designed, I felt I'd passed another big test. "Let go and let God" — it worked!

Years later, a prophet named John Mark came to our house for lunch. When he arrived, he commented on how strong the presence of God was in our home. I told him about how we had relinquished our new house to go to BRSM in Pensacola, Florida. At that point, he began to prophesy about how God wanted to know if we would give Him everything and that we had passed a huge test. God now knew that we would not hold anything back from Him. He needed to test us because of what He would be pouring out on our lives in the years to come. I felt humbled and grateful at the thought of passing my God test.

Song: "I'd Rather Have Jesus," by Selah.

Song: "Lord Let Your Glory Fall," by Matt Redman.

16.
RETURN TO A CHANGING WORLD

Two months after returning to Oregon, I received an early-morning call on September 11, 2001. The caller reported the shocking news that there had been terrorist attacks on America. I was stunned to learn that a group of al-Qaeda Islamic extremists had hijacked four airplanes and carried out suicide missions on targets in the United States. Millions of Americans were suddenly living in a horrific, surreal nightmare. Hijackers had flown two planes into the Twin Towers of the World Trade Center in New York City, causing their collapse. A third plane crashed into the Pentagon just outside Washington, DC. A fourth plane crashed in a field in Pennsylvania. Americans witnessed the worst terrorist attacks in our country's history.

When I heard the news, I remembered an open vision I'd had the previous year during an early-morning prayer time at school. I saw the United States Capitol building with huge fireballs rolling through the hallways and then exploding in its rotunda and other interior spaces. It was a shocking scene that took my breath away when I envisioned it. On 9/11, was the intended target of United Airlines Flight 93 the U.S. Capitol building in Washington, DC? Most likely, Flight 93 was headed for a different target, but was diverted to a field in Shanksville, Pennsylvania, due to the intervention of Todd Beamer and other courageous passengers.

I am looking at Todd's handsome face on my iPhone as I write this chapter. I remember his famous last words, "Let's roll," spoken just before he and a few others prepared to storm the cockpit and take control of the plane. Todd's wife, Lisa, was only five months pregnant the morning of the attack. She bravely gave more than two hundred media appearances during the next six months. Lisa also started the Todd M. Beamer Memorial Foundation in her husband's honor (later renamed "Heroic Choices"), to help children who suffered from trauma. Lisa Beamer did not remarry and has raised her three children alone. I was reminded on 9/11:

> *"The battle line between good and evil*
> *runs through the heart of every man."*
> — *Aleksandr Solzhenitsyn, Novelist*

On September 11, Americans on the West Coast woke up to tragedy. I missed being with the students at BRSM and members of the Brownsville Assembly of God Church. I knew they were all gathered for prayer at that very moment. I recalled the night I wept while lying on the carpet by the "Revival in America" banner during a prayer service. That distressing morning, I felt isolated and separated from my classmates and other prayer warriors.

Tim was at work, and I was alone at Lewisburg Hall without TV or Internet service. I immediately called my father in California. Dad was retired from American Airlines, whose Flight 11 was the plane that struck the north tower of the World Trade Center. I knew that Dad would have insight about the tragic events and would offer wisdom and comfort, like he had many other times in my life. The first thing he said to me was, "I've flown that route." He explained that he had an opportunity to operate a flight simulator at American Airlines. One of the approaches into John F. Kennedy International Airport in New York City went right by the Twin Towers in Manhattan. It was easy to see how the hijackers could have been trained for their evil, destructive plot.

We later learned that a total of 2,996 people were killed in the 9/11 attacks, which included the 19 evil terrorist hijackers. That figure also included 343 firefighters and paramedics, 23 NYPD officers, and 37 Port Authority police officers attempting to complete an evacuation of the buildings and save workers who were trapped on the higher floors. At the Pentagon, 189 people were killed, and 64 people died on American Airlines Flight 11 when the airliner struck the towers. And on United Airlines Flight 93, 44 people died when the plane believed to be headed for a target somewhere within Washington, DC, was diverted by passengers before crashing in a Pennsylvania field. God heard their cries.

In my distress I called to the Lord;
I cried to my God for help.
From his temple he heard my voice.
My cry came before him, into his ears....
— Psalm 18:6

The events of 9/11 marked a time when life as we knew it changed for the people of the United States. Careful screenings at airports and railroad depots were heightened. Personal and national security felt more threatened than ever before, even for someone like me, who had flown on airplanes all of my life. To face the fears and meet the challenges that the attacks caused, the prayers of many people increased. Church attendance in the United States was up temporarily but unfortunately dropped off again. My faith was an anchor in the storm that raged around me. I talked to the One I knew I could depend on.

Is anyone among you in trouble?
Let them pray.
Is anyone happy?
Let them sing songs of praise.
— James 5:13

Song: "I Will Carry You," by Michael W. Smith

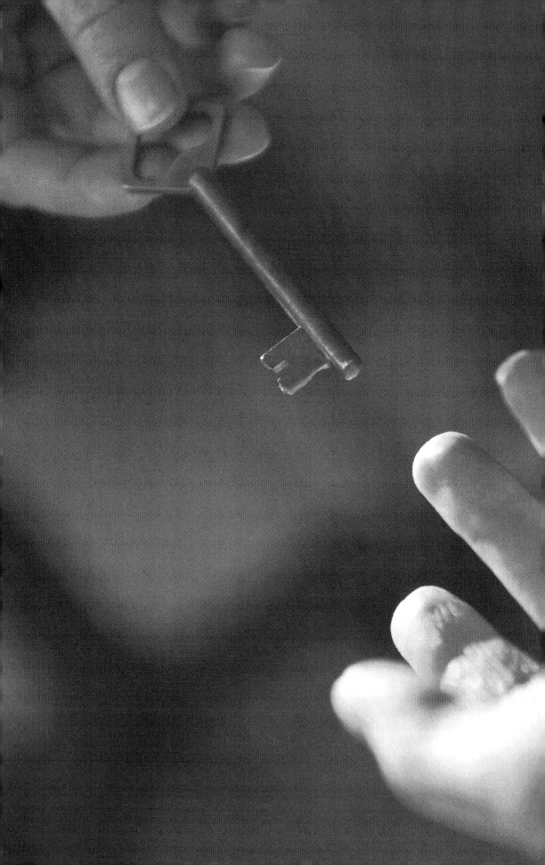

17.
FOR SUCH A
TIME AS THIS

Each of us is here for our appointed time in history, to make our individual contributions. After the events of September 11, I had an increasing desire to live with greater passion and purpose. I trusted there was a Master plan for my life. I was committed to being intentional about discovering and living my destiny to the fullest, for all the days planned for me.

> *Your eyes saw my unformed body;*
> *all the days ordained for me were written*
> *in your book before one of them came to be.*
> — *Psalm 139:16*

For the next nine months, I continued managing Lewisburg Hall. After a seven-year restoration, followed by another seven years of hosting almost eight hundred events, I sensed it was time to let go. I hoped that someone would buy my baby who would love her like I had. I was privileged to be her caretaker for my appointed time in history.

Each December, I held an open house to fulfill the requirement of buildings listed on the National Register of Historic Places. I had two weeks of fun decorating Lewisburg Hall with friends as we drank hot cider, ate cookies, and played Christmas music. She looked so pretty dressed in her holiday décor and provided a welcoming ambience for dozens of holiday gatherings.

In December of 2002, Father Stephen of St. Anne Orthodox Church came to my open house with one of his church members, also a realtor. When they walked into the upper room, Father. Stephen's eyes looked happy. His expression reminded me of how I felt the first time I fell in love with the Hall. Their interest was obvious. After their tour, they told me they were looking for a new church home and asked if their members could meet there. I welcomed them and prepared the dining room for their visit.

Before I left that night, I sat alone downstairs in the warm glow of the Christmas lights. I was surrounded by the memories of all the people who had come. As I took time to give thanks, tears flowed from my tender, grateful heart.

When the members of St. Anne were gathered, Father Stephen asked me to share some of my stories. I told them about the day I first saw the Hall and purchased her. I shared a few highlights about the restoration. I gave thanks for the generous contributors and, of course, the unexpected provision of the "baby money," a key to completing the renovation. The church members were enthusiastic about Lewisburg Hall and voted that day to purchase her. I was happy to see they already loved my baby. They were the people I had hoped and prayed for.

The day St. Anne Orthodox Church became the new owners, Father Stephen's wife, Mona, cried as she came through the front door because she was so happy. As I reflected on all God had done for me and through me, I cried going out the door. My baby had been beautifully restored, and so had I. All my needs were abundantly provided for: the finances, physical strength, encouragement, restoration team, super staff, and great clients.

One of my favorite things to do during events was to sit on the front porch and enjoy the sights and sounds of the people inside. Through the windowpanes, I could see the evergreen garland draped from the beam down the center of the room. Adorned with little white lights, it brought an ambient glow to the room. As I listened to the hum of conversation and the laughter of my guests, I felt happy to have restored a place that the community would continue to enjoy. People of all ages shared happy times at Lewisburg Hall. Their events live on through their photographs, videos, and in my memory.

An Answer to Prayer

About ten years before I sold Lewisburg Hall, my husband and I had watched a teaching by financial advisor Larry Burkett. He encouraged people to pay off their debts and home loans. We were intrigued with the idea of being mortgage free within ten years, but we never actually wrote out a plan to achieve that goal. The day I received payment for the sale of Lewisburg Hall, we drove to the bank, and I wrote out a check that paid off the balance of our home mortgage. That eventful day was about ten years after we first heard Larry's teaching.

"We shape our buildings; thereafter they shape us."
— *Winston Churchill*

*Looking back, you will celebrate the
many opportunities you had.*

18.
BUILD IT, AND
THEY WILL COME

Just this week, I visited Lewisburg Hall, now St. Anne Orthodox Church, for their Greek festival — an annual event to raise funds for the ongoing restoration of the building. Warm, nostalgic feelings were stirred in my heart as I walked toward the Hall. The community came together for Greek food, music, dancing, and celebration. Being there brought back sweet memories of the restoration, my talented team of helpers, and many memorable events we hosted. It was hard to believe my own adventure had begun there almost three decades before.

The people of St. Anne Orthodox Church have owned the building for more than seventeen years. As I walked inside, it seemed like just yesterday that she was mine. Since I served at many events, it took some restraint not to start clearing tables. After sharing hugs and taking a few pictures, I bought some baklava and made my exit, as flashbacks of former years flowed through my memory. It was not easy to let her go. I felt thankful and happy to see all the people enjoying the place we had worked so long and hard to preserve. My baby lives on, as a wonderful place for people to gather and celebrate. I am grateful that my Lewisburg Hall story had a happy ending and that I've left a legacy!

Enter his gates with thanksgiving and his courts with praise;
give thanks to him and praise his name.
— Psalm 100:4

In the spring of 2002, after the sale of Lewisburg Hall, my life entered a new season. It is commonly called "retirement," but I decided to call it my "refirement." It was my time for getting "refired up" about life! For eighteen years, I had been busy with jobs, restoration projects, house designing and building, running a business, and discovering new dreams to replace my unfulfilled desire to be a mother. My role as a community contributor was also part of my new identity. In the midst of all my busyness, I had not thought beyond what I was currently doing to seriously consider my future. I was content just working through my lists. In the meantime, I developed a passion for architecture and historic restoration projects. It was a great run.

We purchased our five lovely acres of property years before we could afford to build there. After a fourteen-year wait, in 1998 we finally built our dream house, a turn-of-the-century-style farmhouse that I had the joy of designing. Throughout my life, I'd had many opportunities to discover new interests and redefine myself. When I entered my "refirement" years, my days became less community-centered and more solitary and home-based. When we moved into our "dream house," thoughts of motherhood bubbled up in my heart again. I'd created the home where I had always imagined raising my children. For years, my busyness, volunteering, multi-tasking, and major projects were my main activities. When I moved to our peaceful country setting, the days mellowed, and time could pass without my cell phone ringing even once.

My new life was healthier and more balanced. With fewer demands and appointments, I no longer needed refill pages for my

Franklin planner. Life was more spontaneous and serendipitous. I enjoyed developing our home's landscape and decorating its interior. As a passionate preservationist and designer, I consulted with others on their historic-building and interior decorating projects. For years, my wall calendar and Franklin planner had dictated how I spent my time. I loved being free to choose which activities filled my days. And I loved putting a big "X" on my calendar for a "play day" or just sleeping in.

Home became my refuge and a welcoming place to share with others. We hosted friends and family from around the U.S., as well as India, Italy, Mexico, Nepal, Norway, and South Korea. The same peaceful presence we had experienced at the Hall and revival continued to reside with us. My country setting was the ideal place to renew my overworked body. Our country yard provided fresh air, exercise, and beautification projects. One of my life mottoes was: "Make it beautiful."

When I stepped out of the public arena, I realized I was actually more of an introvert than an extrovert. As I alternated my busy days with time for solitude and quiet reflection, I found my new groove, and I began to thrive.

You are not what you DO, but who you ARE.

When my life transitioned, I had to fight the temptation to be a doer again and regress to the crazy busyness of my former years. It was my time to break old patterns. "Simplify" became my new favorite word. My major burnout had taught me the importance of maintaining healthy boundaries and being wise in setting reasonable goals. It took me almost ten years to recover from chronic fatigue. I finally gave myself permission to take care of me. I liked feeling vibrant and had no desire to feel like an old lady again while I was still young. I began to see myself as young and energetic.

The Lord will guide you always;
he will satisfy your needs in a sun-scorched land
and will strengthen your frame.
You will be like a well-watered garden,
like a spring whose waters never fail.
— Isaiah 58:11

Life is a marathon, not a sprint.
Find your sustainable pace so you can go the distance.

As I began living peaceably, my health gradually improved. I enlisted the help of a supportive naturopathic doctor and adopted an anti-inflammatory food plan free of gluten, sugar, dairy, chemicals, and preservatives. I discovered food allergies and learned to eat correctly to experience my best health.

For years, I ran on my adrenaline and pushed myself too hard. The coffee and diet caffeinated soda I consumed provided only temporary, fake energy and poisoned my body. In the end, I became more depleted and robbed myself of the health and stamina I needed to run the marathon called life. My new goal was not just to survive — it was to thrive. I became lighter and freer when I lost the excess weight I was carrying and the emotional baggage connected to my past disappointments, hurts, and failures. I reminded myself of this verse:

> *For my yoke is easy and my burden is light.*
> *— Matthew 11:30*

To restore myself and relieve stress, I chose good nutrition, regular exercise, pure water, and fresh air. I wished I had made health changes earlier in life. Studies showed that healthy living and reduced stress could also increase a woman's fertility. During my chronic-fatigue years, my body did not have enough energy to process even its monthly cycle, and my menstrual periods ended altogether, taking with them any hope of my future children.

We ARE what we eat. Choose wisely from life's buffet.

Infertility had brought me down both emotionally and physically. My energy was depleted. I really needed quality food, but I had almost no "oomph" for healthy meal planning or cooking. I lost interest in food altogether. Unfortunately, my entire system was so depressed that I had gained forty pounds. I was at my heaviest weight ever, and I felt lousy. When I crashed and nearly burned up, I had a choice: live in a depressed state or start contending for my own health.

My condition did not improve simply by receiving healing in a prayer line at church. My worn-out condition was my opportunity to partner in my own recovery by choosing a healthy life, one baby step at a time. I did not always do health perfectly, but I gradually learned to love my body, my temple of the Spirit, and to get back on track when I strayed. I showed appreciation for my body by giving myself the tender, loving care it needed.

I praise you because I am fearfully and wonderfully made;
your works are wonderful, I know that full well.
— Psalm 139:14

As I took responsibility for own restoration, my life was gradually rebuilt. In the end, it was a blessing that my health failed, because I had an opportunity to become a much better me, from the inside of my cells to my smile. I adopted the motto: "Do the best you can with what you have." I was never going to be thirty again, but I could still be vibrant. I envisioned a stronger, healthier version of myself. I learned the value of organic food, natural supplements, fitness, regular sleep, deep breathing, and how the mind, body, and emotions are interconnected. I adopted a new, well-rounded approach to my health and maintained a life of prayer that supported an optimistic outlook on life.

As I type this, I feel grateful again for my physical turnaround. Small, positive choices made consistently helped me to reclaim my health. Deborah, my ND, said my recovery was successful because I was ready and willing to make changes. I have been blessed to have her as my health coach, cheerleader, and friend for almost a decade. I am thankful for all the people on my "Support Team" who helped me succeed at life. They know who they are.

When I learned to take care of my health, my life began to flourish. No, I did not get to have my baby, but, one day at a time, I got better, and my hope increased. My outlook was brighter. I understood that I was destined for specific purposes.

Along the way, life happened.

In my life, a little rain always fell. Life's unexpected events came: a loved one got ill, a friend was in need, and disasters hit homes and towns. When the stuff of life happened, the stronger me was better able to handle the demands and unforeseen events. I learned that my capacity to deal with crisis was not static but always changing. Life was always a balancing act. I learned that I functioned best in the place of peace. I found there was always an "eye" in the middle of the storms. As I searched for and found the serene center, I heard His still, small voice more clearly.

Creating a beautiful, healthy home was also important to me. I realized the blessing of having a peaceful refuge, for me and for those I loved. One busy day I was reading my Bible, and Psalm 23 was highlighted for me:

> *The Lord is my shepherd, I lack nothing.*
> *He makes me lie down in green pastures.*
> *He leads me beside quiet waters,*
> *He refreshes my soul.*
> *— Psalm 23:1-3*

Wanting to respond to the Psalm, I went out to our meadow, spread out a blanket, and lay down. As I meditated on the verse, "He makes me lie down in green pastures," I fell asleep. I woke up a couple of hours later feeling peaceful and relaxed, unconcerned about the bugs and little field mice that might have crawled onto my blanket with me. My friend Liz called from Southern California to see what I was doing. She was probably calling from her car phone as she maneuvered six lanes of traffic. Liz laughed when I said I was watching the meadow grow.

I pursued peaceful moments in nature's beauty around me and guarded my place of rest. Let us, therefore, make every effort to enter that rest. (Hebrews 4:11) I watched hummingbirds feeding on my magenta fuchsia and giggled as baby deer frolicked on our hillside. I delighted in magnificent double rainbows decorating the sky and puffy animal shapes in clouds floating by. I was nurtured by gentle walks in the moonlight with a loved one and gazing at bright stars overhead. It was important to practice the art of stillness. It is where I heard best. I discovered His quiet voice. Too often, the noise and distractions of life had threatened to drown Him out. For me, being led by Holy Spirit continued to be a theme in my life and the desire of my heart.

After the earthquake came a fire,
but the Lord was not in the fire.
And after the fire came a gentle whisper.
— 1 Kings 19:12

My life moved deeper into stillness: from loud to quiet, from too busy to calm, from speaking before many to communicating with my One. When life was full of juggling "to do" lists, I was left with little capacity for much else. In rest, ribbons of creativity flowed into my heart and mind. I once lived in a place of striving. Later I learned to surf and go with the flow and listen. Adjustments were needed, and they were oh, so good. Like a baby gosling tucked under her mother goose's wing, I stayed close to Him. I lived in anticipation of receiving important moments and not missing them. I needed peace. I continually chose peace.

Don't strive. He will complete the good work in you.

I was thankful I discovered the importance of living a spirit-led life. Home became my quiet place for reading, writing, and nurturing my spirit. I filled dozens of journals with reflections and teachings. As I transitioned to a gentler life, hidden longings for a child resurfaced again. Rather than focusing inwardly, I expanded my vision to include the needs of others. When I did, I saw opportunities to connect with a stranger at the store. I noticed the one person sitting alone at church. I greeted the neighbors walking by while I was out gardening. Opportunities to love people always presented themselves.

Next to our main mailbox, we had a "Prayer Requests" box. One day when my doorbell rang, I opened the door and a woman asked, "Can I give you a prayer request?"

"Yes, you can. How can I pray for you?" I replied.

She had tears in her eyes as she told me about her 35-year-old son who was going to have heart surgery the following week. After we prayed together, she seemed more peaceful and less worried. I realized that, when I made myself available, He could even send someone to my front door who needed love. I thought, How brave that mother was to knock on a stranger's door and ask for prayer for her son.

For years, I spent quiet time in my "blue room." Its bay window overlooked the street, so I often asked the Holy Spirit to encounter people as they walked on the road in front of our house. I later met Debbie at church, who reported that, as she walked by my house, she noticed our "Prayer Requests" mailbox. She imagined some young girl walking to the mailbox to get the requests. Each time Debbie came to our property line, she would feel the Spirit fall on her. By the time she got to the opposite property line, she would sometimes be crying. Then the presence would lift. She even sat on a power box in front of my house one time and wept.

When she told her husband, Ben, about her experiences, he wanted her to take him there, too. But she said, "No, it's my special place." One day when Tim and I were returning from church, Debbie saw us and realized that we were the "Dodsons" on the mailbox. That's when she told me about her encounters with the Holy Spirit. It encouraged me to hear how my prayers had been answered.

Through my quieter, more prayerful time of life, I surrendered myself to the work of His hands and went through a pruning, shaping, and maturing process.

I am the true vine, and my Father is the gardener.
He cuts off every branch in me that bears no fruit,
while every branch that does bear fruit, he prunes
so that it will be even more fruitful.
— John 15:1-2

Love may disappoint us, but choose love anyway.

When my husband's son and family moved from New York to Oregon, I enjoyed spending time with their two young girls. In the following years, another boy, girl, and boy came into their family. A little red wagon, a tricycle, and a three-ring rubber swimming pool were added to our country yard. Indoors, they played with books, handmade wooden toys, puzzles, and a pile of soft child-sized blankets that I made. I hosted campfires, sleepovers, birthday parties, and extravagant holiday celebrations. As a former preschool teacher, I knew what brought delight to children.

Extra bedrooms accommodated a luxurious canopy bed and miniature Christmas trees. Our cozy upstairs space became a children's room. There was nothing quite like the squeal of little girls running through lawn sprinklers and feeling their arms wrap lovingly around my neck. They had wonderful curiosities and asked great questions. We taught them to garden, cook, ride a bicycle, and eventually drive a stick-shift truck, just to name a few of our exploits.

"I've learned that people will forget what you said, people will forget what you did, but people will never forget how you made them feel."
— Maya Angelou

For many years, Christmas had been a difficult holiday for me. During my childhood, it was a time to be enjoyed with family, especially young children. I always felt there should be surprises and fun activities for kids, but I never had children of my own to celebrate with. When they came into my life, I was more motivated to decorate for Christmas. I anticipated their joy seeing our huge tree filled with tiny white lights and shiny glass ornaments, and surrounded with presents. Christmas felt less empty and more complete. I delighted in their eagerness to bake cookies, scoop ice cream, and even wash dishes. They loved the fun times we created for them.

One Christmas evening as the grandchildren were leaving, I overheard the youngest girl say, "That's the best house in the whole world!" That enthusiastic sentiment was why I did what I did for them. It warmed my heart to find their sweet "Thank you" notes and poems on my bedside table. They always looked forward to coming again. The children were a source of love and joy in my life.

I have cherished the wonderful times and photographs from those years. Then I experienced deep sorrow when their time in Oregon ended. When they suddenly moved back to New York, our family time turned from glad to sad and ended with brokenness. My heart felt an empty place that the children had temporarily filled for more than a decade. Fences were somewhat mended, but time moved on, and our relationships were never the same after that. Families are not perfect, and neither is our love. I am thankful to have good memories. I trust that the children remember the joyful times we shared and that they were dearly loved.

Love never fails.
—1 Corinthians 13:8

SCENE 5:
LIFE HAPPENS

And we know that in ALL things God works
for the good of those who love him…
— Romans 8:28

19.
PASSING THE
BATON

When my dad and "Other Mother" moved from California to Oregon in 2005, our family enjoyed having three generations close by. When dad's eyesight failed, he quit driving and building model airplanes. He had a passion and talent for watercolor painting, but his artistic abilities also diminished. Dad and Glenda chose to spend their senior years near the love and support of family. I realized that a generational passing-the-baton time was fast approaching for us all.

Several years later, my mother also moved from Ohio to Oregon. For more than three decades, she had visited family in Oregon. When my stepfather passed away, it was an obvious choice for mom to move closer to her children and grandchildren. My siblings and I helped her move and get resettled. She soon met a lovely gentleman at the senior center. Paul made sure he got mom's phone number that same day. It was sweet to see their relationship quickly develop and to hear her singing their love song: "At last my love has come along/My lonely days are over/and life is like a song." Before long, they decided to marry. It was fun to share Paul and Mary Lou's golden-years wedding day. Sadly, she lost her sweet Paul only nine months later to cancer. As I navigated my own disappointments throughout the various stages of life, I also shared the joys and sorrows of others.

A few years later, my mother received an unexpected diagnosis of Alzheimer's. Her deteriorating language revealed that she was already in the advanced stage. Mom's physical changes were sudden and shocking. She became fearful and vulnerable, and needed help. I became like her mother, and she became my child. My desire was to help mom finish well. Over a six-year period, we moved her six times, each time to a higher level of care. Her devastating disease came without warning and quickly progressed. It was difficult to watch my once-vibrant, capable mother experiencing confusion and sorrow. It was tough to see both of my parents aging and their anxieties increase.

My dad left us first from cancer, and my mom died a few years later. As the baton was passed, my siblings and I mourned the loss of our parents and became the "older generation." It felt strange to have the "kids" taking charge. The passage of time made me a matriarch in my own family. I had never even fully assumed the role of a "mother" and felt I lacked the experience to be a matriarch. Nevertheless, I became one.

As the oldest daughter, I handled many responsibilities for my mom. Throughout her life, she was always a "large-and-in-charge" person, but in her state of deterioration, she needed help. The mother that had polished my little shoes every night needed me to help choose her socks to match her outfits. We shopped for sturdy, flat shoes to help keep her from tripping and falling. I learned that if we did not laugh some, we could have cried about all of mom's difficult changes. It was an emotional time for both of us, so we laughed when we could and had some sweet mother-daughter moments.

*You will have the opportunity to support
your loved ones through some difficult times.*

Parents come saddled with years of memories and treasures. After my mom and dad passed, came the task of distributing all their precious possessions: the letters, photographs, home furnishings, and lovelies. Mom lightened her load along the way by giving special items to her children and grandchildren. I received a lovely china hot chocolate set, a handmade quilt, and crystal pieces — treasures that had belonged to three generations of women in my family line. For decades, I had delighted in the family treasures we had used on special occasions. Oh, the memories our possessions held!

Mom was a lady, and she modeled for others how to be one. She was well dressed and took good care of her pretty clothes and accessories. It was emotional for me to handle and distribute her personal items after she passed. Mom had a big heart and cared deeply for the needs of others. Her main love language was acts of service, and she served others well. Through various organizations, she gave to the betterment of others. In honor of my mom, I washed, folded, polished and thoughtfully distributed her things. I knew she would like knowing I had donated her things to her favorite charities.

My mother was a family event planner. She was the one most responsible for providing airplane tickets to bring us across the country for milestone celebrations. During my visits, she would sometimes turn a lovely treasure upside down to show me a name written on a piece of tape. She asked me to be sure that the named person received that item. Mom's treasures became our treasures.

Because of the many memories attached to her things, handling and distributing family possessions was an emotional finale to our mother-daughter journey. The sharing is still a thought-provoking work in progress.

From his infancy, my dad had been a lifelong collector of memorabilia: his baptism certificates, boxes of letters, photographs, vintage LIFE magazines, records, Kodak slides, and every U.S. Internal Revenue Service tax form he had ever filed. He still had his birth announcement, Boy Scout card, childhood Sunday school records, and the blueprints of the 1953 ranch-style home he designed. Dad's thirty-five-year career in aviation also added model airplanes and other treasures to his collection.

Not long before dad's passing, he played the trombone his father, Almond, had bought for him with $10 payments. It was not just any old trombone. Dad played it when his Redwood City Sequoia High School band marched across San Francisco's Golden Gate Bridge on its May 27, 1937 opening day. As a young girl, I marched around the house behind my daddy as he played "When the Saints Go Marchin' In." His trombone is mine now, unless some budding musician should be added to the great grandchildren in dad's family line. He was a man of many interests: a model airplane builder, photographer, pilot, house designer, watercolor artist, and 1953 MG TF owner and restorer — a few of his many pursuits. Imagine all the belongings such a gifted man left behind. I received dad's art books and supplies. His watercolor paintings are among my most cherished possessions.

As I looked through the photo albums and boxes, I reflected on precious memories. The hours I spent handling possessions caused me to simplify my own accumulation. I had no children to inherit my treasures when I passed. Who would care about the memories that were attached to my personal things? I realized again that my branch on the family tree would eventually end with me. I had produced no new growth. Infertility and childlessness caused different emotional experiences at the various stages of my life.

My husband and I tried for years to complete a Living Trust. When we tried to make decisions about the distribution of our assets, my heart kept getting stuck on my childlessness. It was painful not to have offspring to leave my possessions to. Even though our Trust eventually included some creative disbursement directives, my heart felt unsettled, incomplete, and sad. Like legacy, inheritance was an important matter to me. I had worked hard throughout my life and wanted my blessings to benefit those I loved. I did not know that one day the desire of my heart would bring a happy conclusion to my legacy and inheritance.

The season of life came when I received invitations to the baptisms, graduations, and weddings of the children of my relatives and friends. Honestly, it was difficult to see the dreams of other people coming true, as my dreams slipped away from ever becoming a reality. My own unfulfilled desires resurfaced most intensely at baby showers. I felt like a square peg in a round hole among all the baby clothes, discussions of deliveries, and the girl and boy names being considered. In that pink-and-blue world, I struggled with the sadness of my unfulfilled baby desires.

I was never quite sure what to buy for a newborn. Even the gift-selection process pricked my tender heart. Many times, I just made a deliberate decision to rejoice with each mommy-to-be, as I tried to conceal my own disappointment. I thought I hid my emotions pretty well, but I feared others might see my pain peeking from behind my mask. Since I had a restricted diet, I could not even medicate my emotions with ice cream and a cupcake. I think I could have swallowed down the emotional lump in my throat with a tasty dessert.

Only recently was I finally able to celebrate a baby coming when I attended Amy's baby shower. She and Jason had tried for ten years to have a child. They had given up and were in the process of adopting, when Amy became pregnant with a girl. (Since then, they also had their second child — a precious boy.) Theirs was the miraculous outcome I had hoped and prayed for, but did not receive. It felt good to rejoice with another pregnant woman and not feel sad for myself. I realized that my heart had finally received some much-needed healing.

> *Rejoice with those that rejoice;*
> *mourn with those who mourn.*
> *— Romans 12:15*

***Song:** "Faithful," by Amy Renée Miller*

20.
THERE MUST
BE MORE

I have never been a big fan of routine. If days were too repetitious, I got bored. I always preferred variety and change and enjoyed living spontaneously and being open to new opportunities.

When my church started a three-month "Training for Reigning" (TFR) school of ministry in 2006, I decided to enroll. The timing was right to refocus from life's routines to an expanded purpose. In TFR, I spent my days with other passionate seekers, mostly those in the younger generation. Many of us were in a time of transition. I was free from jobs and major projects. It was a good time for reconnecting my heart and passion to the One who saw all my days before I was even born. Sensing that surprises and new experiences were coming, I asked for the vision of my life to be enlarged.

I loved spending my days with spiritually focused people who were also imagining new possibilities. At the school, we received prophecies from pastors and fellow students. People saw me becoming an author, a spiritual mother, and one who would go to the nations. I did not know if, or when, their words would be fulfilled. I had been a writer, so the "author" hat seemed like a possible fit. Through the years, the title "mother" had carried plenty of emotional charge for me. My goals did not include, however, going to the nations.

Though I had always loved traveling, I never considered myself "the missionary type." Nevertheless, I decided to stay open to being led in ways that were beyond what my mind could imagine.

Years ago, I began compiling my prophetic words in a binder. I enjoyed pondering the meanings and praying about them. I also had a few CDs of prophetic words spoken over me that were thoughtfully recorded by the church staff. I kept my iPhone close at prophetic conferences to record at a moment's notice. I felt His pleasure when I captured prophecies. I believed the Bible was divinely inspired and written by those who documented its truths, promises, and prophecies. When He spoke, I listened. I had learned that some messages were inspired and some were not, and others would take years to come to fruition.

> *Write down the revelation and make it plain on tablets*
> *so that a herald may run with it. For the revelation awaits*
> *an appointed time; it speaks of the end and will not*
> *prove false. Though it linger, wait for it; it will certainly*
> *come and will not delay.*
> *— Habakkuk 2:2-3*

Writing has long been one of my joys. I began as many young girls have, in a little "Dear Diary" whose tiny gold lock and key protected my secret thoughts. I have always been inquisitive and learned from those around me. I filled many pages of my journals with thoughts and the rich teachings of others.

All of my life, I have been a visionary who has dreamed in detailed, colorful images at night. The more rested and peaceful I was, the better I saw as I slept. As I got into bed, I asked for dreams and had a pen and paper ready to record them when I awakened. I looked for the meaning of dreams that inspired me. When I reread my dream journals, I reflected on the hidden messages they contained and the details that would have otherwise been forgotten had I not recorded them. I have dreamed in metaphors and analogies, often about subjects I am interested in, like the restoration of old buildings. As a nature lover, I dreamed about gardens and mountains, oceans, forest trails, and the natural beauty that resonated with my spirit. I loved being a "seer" and have always valued my dreams.

It was super fun to ride on the coattails of my dad's career in aviation. I have enjoyed flying on airplanes ever since I was a baby. The smell of airplane fuel always brought thoughts of visiting his office off the airplane hangar at the San Francisco airport. Whenever I walked across the tarmac to board an airplane, the sounds and smells always rekindled fond memories and caused a rush of excitement. The subject of aviation and traveling were often a theme in my dreams.

I have enjoyed seeing how God speaks. I learned that His dreams were tailor-made. He spoke to me using imagery I could understand. I have pondered my dreams, their mysteries, and intricate details. Dreams were like jigsaw puzzles with pieces waiting to be assembled.

It is the glory of God to conceal a matter;
to search out a matter is the glory of kings.
— Proverbs 25:2

When I took time to search the meaning of my dreams, it seemed I dreamed more. When I recorded my dreams and considered their mysteries, I felt His pleasure. I sometimes had the same dream more than once, which gave me the opportunity to receive new insights and find the deeper meanings I missed the first time. There was a bonus for having healthy sleep patterns. For me, quality sleep = more dreams. Sometimes when I felt like resting, it seemed I also just needed to dream. I could lie down in the middle of the day, fall asleep, and have several dreams. Like panning for gold in a crisp mountain stream, there were precious nuggets to be found in my dreams."

21.
FLOODS WILL COME

In this life, difficulties come. There is a poignant book by Harold S. Kushner called When Bad Things Happen to Good People. Kushner's three-year-old son was diagnosed with a degenerative disease, which meant that the boy would live only until his early teens. Rabbi Kushner was faced with one of life's most difficult questions: "Why, God?" Years later, he wrote his straightforward, elegant contemplation of the doubts and fears that arise when tragedy strikes our lives. His book offers consolation in times of sorrow. I have not suffered the devastating loss of a child, but emotional floods have come in my life: rejection, betrayal, divorce, and childlessness, as I know they have in yours, too.

In December of 2013, I experienced a real flood. After decorating my mother's house for Christmas, she invited me to stay for dinner, but I felt I should leave. When I got home, I entered through the back door to the shocking sight of water cascading from a hole in the ceiling and the floor covered inches deep in flowing water. My dad's watercolor painting was floating face down in the water. I cried out, "Not my daddy's painting!" It was the first watercolor he had given me — a snow scene of a country chapel in Germany where we had visited together. As I picked it up, I heard broken glass sliding out of the frame. I carried the dripping-wet painting to the garage, carefully laid it on the floor, and said a quick prayer, "Lord, please don't let my dad's painting be ruined!"

I ran back inside to see if the fire-suppression sprinklers in our great room ceiling had been activated. Thankfully, all the sheetrock and woodwork appeared to be intact and undamaged. My husband arrived home at about the same time. He studied the situation and went outside to turn the main water line off. Water was dripping from all the recessed lights in the kitchen ceiling and was rushing down the floor vents. The flood had invaded every room on the first floor.

A few days before this disastrous event, we had hosted longtime and new friends for a holiday luncheon to express our appreciation for their friendship. As our house flood worsened by the minute, they were the first people I thought to call. They came quickly armed with shop vacuums and piles of towels to soak up the water. They showed themselves to be true friends, indeed. Lennon and McCartney said it well: "I get by with a little help from my friends."

Water ran down the kitchen walls, across the counters, filling the kitchen drawers. The oven was even full of water. It was hard to decide where to begin. I knew that solid oak floors would not tolerate water for long, so I figured their damage was already irreversible. Furniture was carried to the back porch. Carpeting was pulled back to vacuum up water that had flowed underneath. The guys aggressively dismantled my Christmas sleigh scene on top of the piano and carried it off. Water rushed down floor vents, tearing the heat ducting loose. Later that night, Tim and Larry had the unpleasant job of crawling under the muddy house to reconnect the ducting and get heat flowing into our flooded house.

Our downstairs bedroom, "the blue room," had been my favorite place for quiet time. It was my peaceful spot. That Christmas, I had decided not to have a big tree in our great room, but just a small tree in the blue room instead. It was an inspired decision. I decorated the tiny tree with a few favorite "Old World Christmas" ornaments and kept things simple. At the local antique mall the week before, I had spotted a cute miniature metal child's stove from the 1940s. It tugged on my nostalgic side, so I brought it home as an early "Merry-Christmas-to-me" present. I had placed the vintage toy stove under our small Christmas tree, just how Santa (aka mommy and daddy) left unwrapped toys under our family tree. When I made my old-fashioned purchase, I did not know how symbolic it was and that Santa was already loading a new, adult-sized Jenn-Air stove onto his sleigh for me. Yes, life is full of the unexpected, the good, and the not-so-good surprises.

Your place of prayer could become your place of refuge.

Interestingly, our blue bedroom was the only space downstairs that was not damaged when our house flooded. The floodwaters had crept just under the door a couple feet into the carpeted room and then stopped. I cut out the corner of wet carpet and removed it. The room where I had prayed and worshipped for many years was preserved as a place of refuge in the middle of our crisis. During our house restoration, my prayer room was still my sanctuary.

For seven months, our entire downstairs was a disaster restoration project. It was later discovered that the cause of the flood was a broken fire-sprinkler pipe in our kitchen ceiling that had frozen and then burst. The fire-suppression system that was supposed to protect our home ended up causing all the damage. In the middle of the mess and stress, the workers and noise, I was thankful to have a place of rest. My toy stove has reminded me of "The Year of our Kitchen Flood"!

The first phase of the restoration was the removal of wet, damaged materials. Our fifteen-year-old home had been built when buildings were constructed using glue, screws, and power tools. In our newer home, the pieces did not pull apart easily. It pained me to hear our oak floors being ripped up with crowbars and to see beautiful moldings being damaged in the process. The dream house we had built was being torn apart. In the midst of the ordeal, I remembered to give thanks, especially for our protective insurance company.

Give thanks in all circumstances…
— 1 Thessalonians 5:18

Next came the important drying-out phase. The disaster restoration team brought large heaters and huge fans to circulate the air and prevent the growth of dangerous black mold. The deafening decibels of the blowers and heaters made it sound like we were living on the edge of an enormous waterfall. We slept in our bedroom on the undamaged second floor but had to walk through the downstairs disaster zone many times a day. Dust, nails, dirt from workers' boots, insulation fibers, and wood splinters were everywhere, even on me. Large sheets of plastic separated the upstairs bedrooms from the first floor, but it was impossible to keep the mess confined to the downstairs.

I dusted, swept, and vacuumed many times a day and sometimes retreated to my quiet blue room, where I could rest and breathe. During the restoration, I logged hundreds of hours of labor. My husband went to his job every day and brought work home at night. My art studio was sacrificed for an office space so he could work until late at night.

It was a crazy, busy time, and I was one tired puppy. Surprisingly, my heart stayed peaceful.

Sheetrock installation was a messy, toxic task. The "mud" used to fill the gaps contained cow blood, mixed with other nasty ingredients. Being highly sensitive to chemicals, I tried to avoid exposure, but I felt sick when the fine sanding began. Thankfully, the insurance agent had warned me that living in a house-restoration project could become stressful. She said they would pay for us to stay in a nice hotel anytime; she reemphasized the word nice. During sheetrock installation, I became overwhelmed with the mess and the workers in my home. It was a good time not to have children. I longed for the time we could fully occupy our home, but that time would not come for many months. We went to the Oregon coast for a long weekend, where I escaped the toxic exposure and rested.

Our house disaster gave me a greater compassion for the suffering of many people around the world. Thousands of Syrians fled from war and still live in refugee camps. People in North Korea are held in prisons and work camps, awaiting release from tyrannical leaders and forced labor. The deadly COVID-19 Coronavirus is currently sweeping across one hundred eighty-four nations around the world. Almost sixty thousand homeless people are living on the streets of Los Angeles. As long as our planet spins, there will be suffering, displacement, and the aggression of man against man, woman, and child. The ability to live in peace and to have a place to call "home" is denied to many.

Blessed is the one who perseveres under trial because,
having stood the test, that person will receive the crown of life
that the Lord has promised to those who love him.
— James 1:12

The storms of life come in many forms. Since our house flooded, this world has experienced many natural disasters like hurricanes, earthquakes, fires, mudslides, volcanic explosions, floods, tornadoes, and tsunamis. On the news, we have witnessed catastrophic losses and the displacement of humanity. The homes and neighborhoods of thousands of Hawaiian residents were completely destroyed and buried beneath unstoppable, scorching volcanic lava. Thousands of residents in Northern California were displaced when monstrous fires completely destroyed their property and towns. Entire communities were recently flattened when hurricanes hit Puerto Rico and the Bahamas and caused devastating losses of life and property. Large brush fires ravaged Australia, leaving many homeless and taking the lives of many koalas and kangaroos. My heart ached for the suffering children, the most vulnerable in the middle of all the disasters. I experienced empathy for those who lost loved ones, pets, worldly possessions, and entire communities. On a smaller scale, I understood the distress people experience when disasters strike their lives.

Home was supposed to provide people with a place of refuge, peace, and security, but disasters came. As long as we have breathed, we have experienced them. God has not caused these disasters, but He has used them to work good in us. Our patience was tested and strengthened. We were offered freedom from our dependence on ourselves and from our material possessions. We gained a greater appreciation for our communities and fellow citizens. Perseverance was developed and a deeper trust was nurtured. We witnessed the beauty in people helping one another and adopted an attitude of gratitude for the simplest of our blessings. Life came out of death, and blessings came from hard times.

The entire world is currently under attack as the deadly Coronavirus is claiming hundreds of thousands of lives. Right now, many people are quarantined in their homes as they wait and pray. We face a demon at the door of our nations threatening our lives and everything we have placed our security and trust in. Once again, I have fixed my gaze on the One who holds the whole world in His hands.

Following my house flood, my dad's lovely watercolor painting of a church in Germany that I found floating face down in the water was miraculously spared. There is only one small nick on the corner of the paper where a broken piece of glass pricked its surface — a tiny reminder of its traumatic day. Even his name, "Darrol," signed in ink, is still legible. I replaced the broken frame and added a brass plaque with the following scripture to commemorate the event:

When the enemy comes in, like a flood
the Lord raises a standard against him.
— Isaiah 59:19

Song: "With A Little Help From My Friends," by The Beatles

In this life, you will run into difficulties.

22.
MERRY CRASH-MAS
Note to self: Follow the Spirit's leading!

A year after our December "Merry Christmess" and house flood, I had what I called my "Merry Crash-mas." With the experience of our house flood still fresh in my memory, I literally crashed head-on into another crisis. While driving home after a busy day of errands, the copy-shop girl called to say she had finished my order. I decided to complete just one more task and pick up my copies. You other A-type people know about having a "get-just-one-more-thing-done" tendency.

When I turned my car around and headed back toward town, I was stopped by a red light at a major intersection. When the two lanes next to me got their green arrows to turn left, I drove straight, but my lane still had a red light! A driver coming toward me turned left, causing a head-on collision. Thankfully, our speeds were slow enough that our air bags did not activate. Since I went against a red light, it did not really matter that the other driver's headlights were off and that she was talking on her cell phone.

At the frightening moment of impact, I instantly remembered a vision I'd had earlier in the day. I actually pictured the crash hours before it happened. The vision was a warning of what could happen. Though I wanted to be sensitive to the spirit's leading, I was distracted by the busyness of my day. The vision could have caused me to be more careful while driving. I was disappointed in myself for not staying alert to the warning.

The crash occurred on a dark, rainy night. Steam poured from my car's crushed radiator under its crumpled hood. My vehicle is dark blue, and hers was black. After we collided, our cars were stopped in the middle of a major intersection. We were vulnerable to other cars crashing into us. I jumped out of my car (not the best idea) and ran to the other driver's door to be sure she was not injured. She looked fine but was talking on her cell phone with her car's headlights off. I yelled to her, "We have to move, or we are going to get hit. Let's back out of the intersection!" I drove my car across the street as it steamed and sputtered. The other driver eventually backed out to safety and then turned her car headlights on.

Thankfully, nobody was seriously injured. I was glad there were no children in our cars that night who could have been hurt. My crash reminded me to be attentive to what I see in daydreams, night dreams, and visions. I kept thinking, I saw this event before it happened! A paper air freshener, in the shape of a cross, hung in my car. The promise printed on its surface read:

He will command his angels concerning you
to guard you in all your ways.
— Psalm 91:11

Testimony: "A Divine Interruption," by Michael W. Smith, YT

23.
MY PRAYER

Being the daughter of a father with a career in aviation, I enjoyed the benefits of free airplane tickets while I was still single. Flying has always thrilled me. I have logged thousands of miles in the air. I am a pioneer at heart who has always had a passion for travel and adventure. I expected I would continue traveling throughout my lifetime. I looked forward to retirement, the "Go Years," when I could see more of the world. I learned, however, that my husband was more of a settler and preferred staying closer to home. He is a man of patterns who always said he had no "wanderlust" or strong desire to travel. When he retired from work and his deadlines, commuting, and early-to-bed-early-to-rise schedule, he was content having coffee with buddies, going on fishing trips, working in the yard, reading, and taking naps. As for me, Leonardo da Vinci said it well:

"Once you have tasted flight, you will forever walk the earth with your eyes turned skyward, for there you have been, and there you will always long to return."
— Leonardo da Vinci

I sensed a time of traveling was coming for me. I felt I was being prepared for new places and experiences. My desire was to live every day with passion and purpose, leaving nothing on the table at my life's end. I was not interested in having a predictable, self-focused retired life. And I certainly had no desire to load, unload, and clean a recreational vehicle. I planned to leave my housework behind when I was free to go on worldwide adventures.

One day as I was feeling particularly stuck in familiar scenery and routine, I said this simple prayer: "God, I feel my world is getting too small. Please enlarge my world." My request was spoken much like the prayer of Jabez:

> *Jabez cried out to the God of Israel,*
> *"Oh, that you would bless me and enlarge my territory!*
> *Let your hand be with me, and keep me from harm so that*
> *I will be free from pain." And God granted his request.*
> — *1 Chronicles 4:10*

I knew that the motion picture of my life was written and directed by the One who formed me in my mother's womb. My big-picture Director held my life's script from its "Once upon a time" to "The End." I trusted that He had new discoveries and purposes for me to fulfill. I felt far from my final scene. In anticipation of my upcoming adventures, I made a faith purchase of two cute suitcases and put them up on my closet shelf. As I waited, I wondered where in the world I would be going. I had the feeling my next journey was in the not-too-distant future.

Trust in the LORD with all your heart
and lean not on your own understanding;
in all your ways submit to him,
and he will make your paths straight.
— Proverbs 3:5-6

SCENE 6:
BEYOND ALL I COULD
HAVE ASKED OR IMAGINED

*Finding the gold coin on my walking path was the
start of a new adventure in my life.*

24.
THE COIN

This is where my story takes an unexpected new turn. In the year 2015, my husband and I regularly walked on a path next to the Willamette River, where we observed the riverfront activities of wild geese, ducks, and nesting osprey. In the summertime, the large cottonwood trees provided a protective canopy of shade, and wild blackberry bushes invited tasting. In the autumn, we enjoyed the fall colors.

One January morning, I spotted a pretty gold coin lying in the middle of the path. I was surprised that nobody had seen the shiny coin and taken it. As I picked it up, I heard these words: "I am putting Asia on your path." I asked, What? Asia was not even on the list of places I had considered going. The coin had Asian characters on it and looked brand new. I wondered how it ended up on my small-town path. I felt a stirring inside as I tucked the coin in my pocket.

A few days later, I researched its origin and learned it was a Japanese dime. Each time I came to the spot on the path where I'd found the coin, I remembered the prophetic words, "I am putting Asia on your path," and I pondered their meaning. I felt expectant that something good was about to happen.

I have always had a passion for creating beautiful homes and gardens, but I eventually realized that I experienced even more joy in the envisioning and designing phase of my creations. Country property requires maintenance. I have spent thousands of hours weeding and pruning and have logged many miles on a riding mower. Though I always adored being a beautifier, the responsibility of maintaining my creations sometimes felt weighty. I bought a plaque that said "Simplify" and hung it on my wall. I meditated on the following verse as I considered how to make life simpler:

> *Come to me, all you who labor and are burdened,*
> *and I will give you rest. Take my yoke upon you*
> *and learn from me, for I am meek and humble of heart;*
> *and you will find rest for yourselves.*
> *For my yoke is easy, and my burden is light.*
> *— Matthew 11:28-30*

I have been in the company of talented workaholics all of my life, and at times I was one. After observing my family in operation for many years, my husband coined our mode of intensively tackling our projects as "Davison Disease." During my ten-year recovery from chronic fatigue, I realized that my crammed calendar did not allow me to spontaneously enjoy enough fun or unpredictable opportunities.

Discovering the gold coin on my walking path was just the beginning of a wonderful new adventure in my life. I decided to remain open to life's surprising, serendipitous events. My suitcases were waiting in the wings for their debut.

25.
THE HOOK

Several months after I found the coin, we visited friends in Eastern Oregon for our usual good times with nature walks and late-night talks. One evening, Mark and Marty asked us if we would like to watch a Korean drama. They explained that, in Korea, the dramas were weekly TV programs with simple story lines and multiple episodes. At the end of each episode, there was always a "cliff-hanger" that encouraged the viewer to watch the next show.

Our friends had a lengthy discussion about which favorite drama they should show us. After all, it was going to be our introduction to K-Drama, and they wanted us to have an enjoyable first experience. They decided on You Are Beautiful (YAB), a cute drama about a young pop band whose Korean cast was: Jang Keun Suk, Park Shin Hye, Jung Yong Hwa, and Lee Hong-gi. While watching YAB, my husband and I were not quite sure what to think about Korea's K-Dramas.

As I followed the English subtitles, I became intrigued with the Korean language. The drama featured four young Korean teens in a K-Pop band. When one of the band members went to the United States for a surgery, the band's manager secretly recruited his look-alike sister from a convent to replace him. Without revealing his plan to the band members, the manager secretly groomed the sister to look like her brother and join the band. The K-Drama had a cute plot. I enjoyed watching two episodes; it was my introduction to the K-Drama and K-Pop culture.

When I returned home, I decided to watch the remaining thirteen episodes to see how the light-hearted story ended. I was never an American soap-opera fan, but I knew there was also a "hook" at the end of each show to lure the viewers into watching the next one. Each episode of You Are Beautiful did more than just satisfy my story-line curiosity. My interest in the Korean culture, arts and entertainment industry, cuisine, and the people, particularly their youth, was ignited. The popular Asian K-Drama was the "hook" that first drew my attention to Korea.

In addition to watching the K-Drama episodes, I began doing research. I learned about Korea's challenging educational system, the expectations that were placed on the younger generation to achieve success, and the pressures of their culture. I watched documentaries about how South Koreans rebuilt their country after the devastating Korean War of 1950 to 1953. Their people made significant personal sacrifices, and South Korea had a rapid and remarkable post-war comeback. When visitors came to the Seoul Olympics in 1988, they were impressed when they saw what South Korea had accomplished during the thirty-five-year restoration of their country.

Because their people are South Korean's main resource, they strive to excel, which makes their culture highly competitive. The "V" for victory hand sign, along with their chant, "Fighting," are commonly used. I was shocked and saddened to discover that South Korea has one of the highest suicide rates among the developed nations. As I learned about the hard-working Korean people and the price they paid to conform to cultural expectations, I was moved to pray for them. I saw how their competitive society had created intense stress in their lives.

I had heard the "Seven Mountains" teaching by Lance Wallnau, author and speaker, explaining there are seven mountains, or spheres of culture, where nations are shaped. In 1975, Bill Bright, the founder of Campus Crusade for Christ, and Loren Cunningham, the founder of Youth With a Mission, had lunch together in Colorado. At that lunch, both men were simultaneously given a seven-mountain message to give to the other. The message received by the men was this: In order to impact any nation, we need to influence the seven mountains (7M), or spheres, that are the pillars of their society. The 7M of culture are: business, government, media, arts and entertainment, education, the family, and religion. Several months later, the Christian theologian Francis Schaeffer also received the same message. These men, who were the change agents of a new generation, were all given a strategy for how and where cultures would be won or lost — by conquering the seven mountains.

As I learned about Korea, I felt drawn to pray primarily for the nation's influential arts and entertainment arena. I also prayed for Jang Keun Suk, Park Shin Hey, and a K-Pop band named CNBLUE: with Jung Yong Hwa, Kang Min Hyuk, Lee John Hyun, and Lee Jung Shin. I also focused on the arenas of Korean business and education, particularly how the entertainers influenced the younger generation. While watching my first K-Drama, three young actors from YAB were continually highlighted. I watched other K-Dramas featuring Keun Suk, Shin Hye, and Yong Hwa and saw them as more than actors in dramas; they were, potentially, influential culture shapers among their generation.

I recognized the opportunities for K-Drama and K-Pop to be a positive influence outside of Korea. K-Drama has been exported throughout Asia and to other parts of the world. Whether one sees K-Drama and K-Pop as appealing or not, the success of their multi-billion-dollar industry was undeniable. K-Pop mega stars were featured in the half-time show in the 2018 Olympics in Korea. The Recording Academy's 2019 GRAMMY Awards in the United States also featured the seven-member boy band BTS, who were the first K-Pop band to present an award.

The South Korean film Parasite recently received six nominations at the 2020 Academy Awards and won four Oscars, including Best International Film, Best Screenplay, Best Director for Bong Joon Ho, and the most coveted prize of all, Best Picture. Parasite broke through the "bamboo ceiling" and was the first non-English-speaking film to win the Best Picture Oscar. These honors came in the one-hundredth anniversary of South Korean filmmaking. It was Korea's time.

As I prayed for Korea's entertainment industry, the important questions for me were: How can these Korean actors and their entertainment companies use their platform to positively shape culture and influence the next generation? And how can they stay focused and maintain their integrity? As Lance Wallnau has wisely said, "If you get to the top of your mountain faster than your character, you will expose yourselves to temptations you won't have the ability to overcome." I prayed that the actors and musicians would not miss their culture-shaping opportunities.

Part of my daily quiet time included praying for Korea. I was being drawn to a nation that I perceived was obviously on God's heart. As He began to share His heart with me, I became agonizingly aware of South Korea's tragically high suicide rate among its youth, even those who were part of the K-Pop and K-Drama community. I felt compassion for the younger Korean generation and prayed about the challenges they faced.

26.
PRAYING FOR
THE FAMOUS

Many years ago, two names kept coming to my mind during prayer: John Denver and John F. Kennedy, Jr. I felt nudged to pray for both high-profile young men, which I did for a while. One day, I felt mocked by a voice in my head that asked, "Whom do you think you are to be praying for these famous people?" I was intimidated by the question and eventually quit praying for both Johns. I regretted not being faithful to continue with what I later believed was a prayer assignment.

On October 12, 1997, I was shocked to hear that American singer, songwriter, and actor John Denver, only 53, was killed when the experimental Long-EZ airplane he was piloting crashed off the coast of Pacific Grove, California. After his plane's tank one ran out of fuel, he crashed as he was trying to reach the switch to activate tank two. It seemed like a preventable accident for Denver, who was an experienced pilot.

My father was living in the area at the time. The stretch of coastline in Pacific Grove where Denver crashed was one of our favorite places to sightsee and picnic. On a visit to dad's, he showed me the newspaper articles he had saved about the crash. He knew that Denver was a beloved musician from my generation. As I read the story, it felt like salt was being poured into my wounded heart. Dad did not know I was disappointed in myself for not continuing to pray. I was sure I was not the only one praying for John Denver, but I wondered if he would still be alive had I continued to pray. Perhaps I took too much responsibility. Nevertheless, my regret was deep. Another sad fact was that the tragic death of my beloved Denver, whose songs I had sung and played on my guitar, did not jump-start my prayers for the other John.

On July 16, 1999, I received more tragic news when John F. Kennedy, Jr., only 39, died in a small plane crash in the Atlantic Ocean off the coast of Massachusetts near Martha's Vineyard. He was the other famous "John" I had felt led to pray for. I was shocked at the devastating news. He died, along with his wife, Carolyn Bessette, and her sister, Lauren. Just like Denver, Kennedy died when the Piper Saratoga light aircraft he was piloting crashed into the ocean. From wars, to assassinations, and senseless deaths, my generation suffered the tragic losses of those who died too young.

I remembered John F. Kennedy, Jr., little "John John," the adorable two-year-old son of President John F. Kennedy. He was photographed by UPI photographer Stan Stearns as he saluted his father's horse-drawn casket as it moved down the streets of Washington, DC, following President Kennedy's 1963 assassination. All of these men, three Johns, had died tragically and too young. I felt so overcome with grief the day JFK, Jr. died that I stayed in bed most of the day, crying and feeling sick inside. That day I whispered this vow: "If I ever feel led to pray for famous people again, I will not question your leading."

Eighteen years later, I was reminded of that promise as I began to pray for the young Korean entertainers I had been introduced to through K-Drama and K-Pop. I felt strongly that I needed to fulfill my vow to pray for the famous. To be a loyal prayer warrior, I wanted to be intentional. I went to a local bookbinding business where they made hardbound journals. I purchased one for each entertainer, the band, and the nation of Korea, and had their names embossed on the covers.

My prayer journey drew me deeper into His heart for Korea, where I discovered a new love for the country and her people. Throughout 2016, I prayed daily and wrote my prayer highlights and impressions in the journals. I was often awakened in the night to pray for a people and a country that was 5,250 miles from my Oregon home, a place I had not visited.

John Denver had said that "Perhaps Love" was the best song he ever wrote. On one of his most depressing days, shortly after the death of his father, he was driving up the California coastline. As he drove, he thought about all the people who had loved his music. That night, he penned the following song for his fans. I was told that Koreans loved the song.

Song: "Perhaps Love," by John Denver

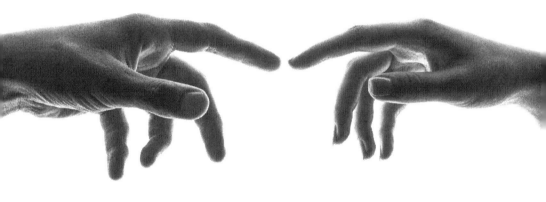

27.
A VISION
OF HONGDAE

One Sunday night in January of 2016, I watched a live-streaming service from Bethel Church in Redding, California. Pastor Paul had arranged a special presentation with a storytelling format. He interviewed four people who each shared their testimony about how a particular desire of their heart had been fulfilled.

> *I remain confident of this:*
> *I will see the goodness of the Lord*
> *in the land of the living.*
> *Wait for the Lord;*
> *be strong and take heart*
> *and wait for the Lord.*
> *— Psalm 27:13-14*

• Amy, a young wife, told how she and her husband, Jason, had tried unsuccessfully for ten years to have a baby. After they quit trying and began the process of adoption, Amy got pregnant. I knew this couple because they were part of my church family in Albany, Oregon. Their infertility journey was definitely a faith-stretching one. I related to their story and was pleased to be among those invited to celebrate her baby's long-awaited arrival at Amy's Oregon baby shower. Amy and Jason eventually had a beautiful baby girl and then a baby boy, too!

• Another woman, Shara, had fasted and prayed about her desire for a husband. In her late thirties, she finally met her future Aussie husband, and they were enjoying a happy marriage. She wanted her testimony to give hope to all the single people.

• A third woman, Libby, told about the financial breakthroughs she and her husband had experienced. After going through a difficult season of poverty and lack, they finally broke through into a life of financial miracles and provision. She encouraged people to remember that they could hope to live an abundant life.

• Ben was an evangelist who'd recently ministered in Europe. He had no qualifications or money but was able to help organize and preach at a major youth gathering in Germany in the same stadium where Adolf Hitler had trained young Nazi soldiers for evil purposes. Ben told about his own, personal, restoration. He had been rescued from a destructive life of drug abuse and was transformed into one who was passionate about inspiring the younger generation. He encouraged the young Army of God to go out and bring hope to a world that needed love.

I loved hearing the testimonies about a miracle baby, meeting a mate, receiving financial provision, and being launched into one's destiny. Each person who shared their story had waited years to receive what they hoped for. They experienced the challenges we all confront when a desire is made to wait: doubt, impatience, and wondering when or if they would receive what they had desired. Their stories were sincere, transparent, and encouraging. They revealed the unique tests of faith they had endured. They knew what it was like to have their hopes deferred and delayed. In time, the desires of their hearts were finally fulfilled. The faithfulness of God in each testimony was unquestionable.

Their encouraging words continued: "Some of you have a big dream, the kind that makes you a little nervous. Can you say, 'I'll go anywhere and do anything'?" They released courage to the people to say, "Yes," whatever the cost.

> *Against all hope, Abraham in hope believed and so became*
> *the father of many nations, just as it had been said to him,*
> *"So shall your offspring be." Without weakening in his faith,*
> *he faced the fact that his body was as good as dead — since*
> *he was about a hundred years old — and Sarah's womb was*
> *also dead. Yet he did not waver through unbelief regarding the*
> *promise of God, but was strengthened in his faith and gave*
> *glory to God, being fully persuaded that God had power*
> *to do what he had promised.*
> *— Romans 4:18-21*

After the testimonies were shared, the worship team began singing this simple chorus: "Holy Spirit, I surrender, I say 'Yes' to you. Jesus. Jesus." I joined in singing with them at home. The service was full of hope. I sensed life was being breathed into the unfulfilled dreams of many people, both in the service and among those watching on the Internet, like I was. I loved saying "Yes" with people all over the world as we worshipped. Ah, the beauty of the Internet that connected us to one another.

My Vision

Toward the end of the service, I began to receive a vision, a clear daydream. I pictured a city scene from the Hongdae district of Seoul, South Korea. I saw a café-coffee house filled with young people and heard the words: "house of prayer" and "training and equipping center." I knew that, in such a place, the young people of Korea could receive encouragement and learn to be friends of God. Hope could replace the desperation that had already caused too many of them to end their lives in suicide. Wanting to capture what I was seeing and hearing, I reached for my journal and quickly began writing down the vision.

During my online research about young Korean entertainers, I had seen an interview with Jung Yung Hwa, the lead singer of the K-Pop band CNBLUE. He recommended that visitors to Seoul, South Korea, visit the Hongdae area, with its cafes, art galleries, musical clubs, and four universities.

After filling a page in my journal with my Hongdae vision, I read it and thought, Hmmm, that's interesting. In the following weeks, I reviewed my journal entry and pondered the meaning of the vision. And I thought about the words I heard the day I found the gold coin on my walking path: "I'm putting Asia on your path."

28.
KOREA: LAND OF CULTURAL EXPECTATIONS

As I learned about the nation of Korea, I was increasingly endeared to the country and her people. South Korea was very poor after the Korean War. They believed that education was the best way for their people to prepare their society and have a successful life. Education is considered one of the biggest treasures in every country. South Korea's educational system is the envy of the world. Pearson, a British multinational publishing and education company, ranked the education in primary, secondary, and high school, as well as the higher-education institutions and international schools in countries around the world. First in their ranking was South Korea, followed by three more Asian countries: Japan, Singapore, and Hong Kong.

I learned that the academic pressure on South Korean students is intense. They pay a high price to be educated in the "Number One" ranked school system in the world. Beginning in junior high school, students spend long days in school. They also go to study labs at night, where there are sometimes people patrolling to keep them awake. They study until quite late before riding the subways home and often go to bed after midnight. In Korea's educational system, the scores on their high school exams determine their futures. As one Korean student said, "When I'm preparing for exams, who I am is just lost." There are four major universities in the Hongdae district of Seoul. Their college students live under extreme stress due to the cultural expectations placed on them to get hired by the best companies. They attend the top schools and receive diplomas from the best universities to give them the opportunity to work for Korean companies like Samsung, Hyundai Motors, Pasco, Kia Motors, and LG.

In the United States Declaration of Independence is the well-known phrase "life, liberty, and the pursuit of happiness" — three examples of the rights the Declaration states have been given to all humans by their creator, and which governments are created to protect. To South Koreans, this probably seems quite idealistic and independent compared to the values esteemed in their culture. The expectation of Korean parents is that their children will achieve success and excellence, which is often measured by a flawless youthful appearance, prosperous jobs, fine cars, and nice homes. Parents often determine what subjects their children should study and which occupations they want them to prepare for. It is challenging for the younger generation to balance honoring their elders with allowing themselves the freedom to pursue what they feel passionate about.

South Korea is one of the plastic-surgery capitals of Asia. For high school graduation gifts, some parents pay for cosmetic surgeries for their students, hoping that an improved appearance will give them a competitive edge. Korean men are handsome, and the women are pretty; in my opinion, few need surgical alterations. When parents direct their young graduates to be chosen for certain universities and specific careers, I think it is possible they ignore the students' individual interests and could thwart their true destinies. Once Koreans do get a job, if they do not perform well, they are simply replaced by younger employees willing to work harder for less money.

The tremendous pressure to succeed has caused South Korea to have the highest suicide rate of growth among youth from ten to nineteen years old. Suicide among fifteen to twenty-four-year-olds is the most common cause of death in Korea. Elderly suicide is also a problem, and poverty is the main cause. The tragic subject of suicide is taboo in Korea and is not talked about much. Suicide is sometimes a shame that requires those who are willing to take up the cause of what has happened in their country. As I learned about Korea's suicide statistics, I was heartbroken.

"Suicide police" patrol District 104 in the heart of the Ceong district to help rescue potential suicide victims. The Mapo Bridge, on the edge of the Hongdae district, is where many desperate young students have yielded to cultural stress and ended their lives by jumping and drowning in the Han River below the "suicide bridge." Koreans have needed wisdom to know how to turn their people from death to life. I prayed that life would flow up and down the streets and into the universities. I asked that the students who struggled with insecurity would find the help they needed to survive their country's competitive environment.

29.
SEASONS
OF SUFFERING

In early 2016, I suffered with severe migraine headaches. They were debilitating and sometimes lasted for several days. I had to lie in a quiet, dark room, usually feeling extreme nausea. But even in my weakness, I could still pray. As I prayed for Korea and the young entertainers, I thought about the Hongdae vision I'd had.

After a week of horrible headaches, my friends Robin and Martha called to ask if they could come pray for me. I appreciated their loving offer and welcomed their prayers. As we spent time praying, the pain in my head greatly improved. Then an intense passion for Korea began to well up inside me. As Life Coach Lance Wallnau said, "Passion gets us into the game to the area of the world we are called to go."

Then I began to see Korean faces and street scenes. I said to my friends, "There is something about Korea." They agreed and said, "Yes, there is. Let's pray about it." As we spent time praying, I recorded in my journal the things we saw and sensed. During our prayer time, more seeds were planted in my heart for Korea that would begin to germinate in the following days and weeks. Our prayer time wonderfully confirmed the feelings I had that I would soon be going on an adventure to another country. That day, I was pretty sure I would be going to Korea.

I had never imagined what God was preparing for me to do, and neither can you!

He has shown the people the power of his works,
giving them the lands of other nations.
— Psalm 111:6

30.
BIRTHING KOREA
IN PRAYER

In January of 2016, I had my first vision of Korea. In March, I received confirmation when I was praying with my friends. My "spiritual midwives" supported me as I birthed the vision. When I shared my quickly developing experience with other friends, they also began praying for me. Wisdom, discernment, and guidance were needed, as the vision was aligned with my destiny. I wanted to love people and carry hope to where it was needed and to protect the mission from being aborted. Some things in this life have been worth fighting for, and my Korea vision was one of them.

> *"Let's make sure that, when God offers us cities, mountains, industries, nations, vast amounts of money, and influence, we don't back away from the invitation because we're not sure we can do it."*
> — *Lance Wallnau, Author*

At our March prayer time, I brought my prayer journal with the Hongdae vision I had recorded two months earlier. I read my friends the vision and welcomed their feedback. I knew they loved me enough to say if they thought the vision was my own imagination or not. After I read the journal entry, Robin emphatically said, "That's God." She explained that through the years she had heard many stories and visions and that she just "knew in her knower" that my Korea vision was from God.

We had a rich prayer time that day. An impression, a word of direction, a scripture, and something that moved my heart — one colorful thread at a time, a beautiful tapestry began to be woven. My wise friends confirmed things I had seen during my quiet time and had written in my journal. At that point, my adventure shifted into a higher gear. I was thankful for the prophetic words that were given. I felt stirred up, built up, and cheered up. Before long, I felt my unborn Korean "baby" kicking inside me.

And it shall be in the last days, God says,
that I will pour out my spirit on all people.
Your sons and daughters will prophesy,
your young men will see visions,
your old men will dream dreams.
Even on my servants, both men and women,
I will pour out my Spirit in those days, and they will prophesy.
—Acts 2:17-18

The luggage I'd purchased in faith awaited its maiden voyage. When I saw it up on my closet shelf, I felt I would be going to Korea soon. One day during prayer, I asked, "When will I be going to Korea?" and I heard "October." I wanted to put my feet in Korea, to experience the culture, and get to know the people. I pictured myself looking out a window of a downtown high-rise hotel as I prayed over the city of Seoul, South Korea. During quiet times and in my night dreams, I received prayer strategies for my trip. Some mornings when I woke up, I heard myself praying out loud for Korea. I was definitely being drawn to a new country, and I spent time "pre-prayering" in advance.

When my friends and I prayed in April, we received more details for my first trip to Korea. We prayed about the team I would go with. During prayer that day, I envisioned a tall male standing on a busy street corner in Korea, wearing a burgundy sweater. I was impressed with his height, because he was taller than most of the medium-sized Korean men I had seen in the K-dramas, K-pop bands, and interviews I had watched.

The moment I saw him, I knew in my knower that he was someone who was going to help me on my first trip to Korea. Some visions and night dreams fade with time, but the one I saw of that Korean man is still crystal clear. My vision was a preview of things to come. One day I would be sure that I was in the right place, at the right time, with the right person.

There is a time for everything,
and a season for every activity
under the heavens.
— Ecclesiastes 3:1

31.
SEARCHING
FOR MY TEAM

Who would I travel to Korea with? I needed to find my people, those with kindred spirits and the same assignment. Though my husband reluctantly said he would go if I could not find anyone else, I knew he did not enjoy traveling. Another friend had prayed for Korea for several years and considered going but decided she did not feel called. I understood the importance of being called to a place at our appointed time.

> *...in all your ways submit to him,*
> *and he will make your paths straight.*
> — *Proverbs 3:6*

My friend remembered that her sister had attended a conference in Anaheim, California, that she thought was held at a Korean church. That week, I looked online for a Korean church in Anaheim. I also found the schedule of the conference speaker. I was hopeful when I saw that James had spoken at Blessed International Church (BI) in Anaheim the past March. I searched for and found BI. When I saw Pastors Ryan and Joann and other

Korean faces among the staff pictures, I sensed I had tapped into my gold vein.

Feeling hopeful, I sent Pastor Ryan an email that same day. I told him I was a woman in Oregon interested in taking my first trip to Seoul, South Korea. I briefly shared the vision I'd had of the Hongdae district, and I asked if they sent mission teams from their church to Korea. The next day, I received an enthusiastic response from Pastor Ryan with several "Wows" and exclamation marks. He said their church was planning to send Janet to Korea, to plant a café/house of prayer in Hongdae and that a team from their church was going to Seoul in October, the same month I thought I would be going.

I was expectant that I had found my team. Pastor Ryan asked me if I would consider flying to Southern California to meet them and Janet, their first missionary to Korea. He explained that just two days before I sent him my email, a lady in their church had prophesied to Janet that God would send a woman who would be joined heart to heart with her to help with her ministry in Korea. God orchestrated what I could not have on my own. I agreed to go meet them, and I made a plane reservation to fly to California two weeks later.

I called Robin and Martha to tell them about my email exchange with Pastor Ryan. I was encouraged by Robin's response: "Everything you have done up until now has been good, but this is what you were born for and what you will be doing for years to come." Something new was being birthed in me. My "Wow Adventure" had officially taken off!

Two weeks later, I took a Jet Blue flight to Long Beach, California. I sat in seat 9E next to a lovely Korean lady named Young Mi, sitting in seat 9D. She asked me why I was traveling to Southern California, and I briefly shared my story. "Wow!" she said. Then she began to tell me about her 30-year-old son who encountered God when he was in Mongolia with Youth With a Mission (YWAM). His dream was to help start a cashmere business for women in Mongolia to help pull them out of sex trafficking. But since his return to the US, she said he was partying too much. She said my story inspired her to draw closer to God and trust Him with her family.

Young Mi was full of Bible promises. She quoted verses about how her family would be saved from their troubles. She also shared verses with me from Genesis about how Abraham went out, not knowing where He was going. I could relate to that story. As I shared my testimony, I saw how the people around me were warmed by His encouraging love. I realized that my story was meaningful, even in its infant stage.

When I arrived in Long Beach, my sister picked me up at the airport. It was good to have family living there who would share in the genesis of my "Wow journey." When I arrived at Sherri's house, my room had a strong smell of varnish from carpentry work done earlier that day. Being highly sensitive to chemicals and odors, I knew I would not be able to sleep there without getting sick. I could not begin my adventure with a migraine headache.

After sharing our first dinner at my sister's favorite Korean restaurant, we found a simple hotel room for me close by. I felt lonely at first, but in the days to come, I realized that my private room was just where I needed to be to process my new adventure. And there was something significant about me starting my adventure solely dependent on Him. In that hotel room, I felt the prayers of family and friends covering me. As I experienced all that was happening, I prayed, wrote, and rested. In that cocoon of God's presence, my new metamorphosis began. It was an intense and humbling time.

My first morning in California, I took an Uber taxi to Blessed International Church to meet Pastors Ryan, Joanne, and Janet. On our ride, my driver asked me, "Why are you in Southern California?" I had my second opportunity to tell about the events that were unfolding in my life. Even though my adventure was just beginning, I saw again that my story sparked something in my male Uber driver. He told me about a dream he had to help people through a financial-management business he was hoping to start. He asked me lots of questions and kept saying, "Wow, this is a really good story!" He said he was excited for me, and he wished me well. I was happy to see that he was inspired, too. As he drove off, I imagined my driver was probably thinking about his financial business. I was reminded that many people have dreams. I could see that sharing my story had sparked my driver's dream. I prayed that he would pursue and successfully fulfill his desires. Needless to say, his enthusiasm caused my own excitement to build.

Minutes later, I met Janet. When we shared our first hug, I felt a uniting of spirit and purpose. Pastor Joanne greeted me with a warm, welcoming smile. I think we all felt that our connection was God-guided. Janet and I shared our first lunch at an umbrella table in the warm California sunshine. We took turns telling about how our paths had led us to that moment. It was fun to see how God's purposes and timing had been at work in our lives. I remember saying "Wow!" many times. My cheeks got sore from smiling so much.

One of the interesting things I learned when we talked was that Pastor Joanne, Janet, and I all had house floods at the same time. We each experienced the disruption that disasters bring and went through the process of having our homes restored. I was not quite sure what to think about that coincidence, but our common experience definitely piqued my interest. Somehow, our house floods were part of our preparation.

I enjoyed meeting Janet, a creative young Korean-American woman, who had been prepared to be Blessed International's first missionary to Korea. When I shared my story about how my heart had been drawn to Korea, she also kept saying "Wow!" Interestingly, we both expressed that part of our preparation had been to watch K-Dramas, even though we wondered at the time whether we were being distracted by something meaningless. Somehow the dramas had tenderized our hearts and turned our attention toward Korea.

The next day, we all met together. We worshipped, shared our stories, and prayed. I brought my journal that contained the Hongdae vision that I had recorded four months earlier. When I read them my vision, they kept saying "Wow!" They revealed that they had received a similar vision for the Hongdae outreach while spending time in their church's House of Prayer. They had been discussing and praying about the mission for quite some time, and they seemed encouraged.

For we are God's workmanship,
created in Christ Jesus to do good works,
which God prepared in advance for us to do.
— Ephesians 2:10

I enjoyed connecting with my sister in the evenings for dinner and telling her how events were unfolding. One afternoon she took me to a shopping center in Fullerton, California, with Korean restaurants, shops, and a large supermarket. About 30,000 Koreans lived in her city. In a small shop on the edge of the grocery store, I met Susie at her store, "My Treasure." I asked her if she had any Korean Bibles, but she did not. She did, however, say that she had a Korean-English Bible at home that she wanted to give me to support my work as a "missionary" in Korea. That was the first time that anyone had ever called me a "missionary." My first Korean-English Bible was a precious gift from Susie, my new Korean acquaintance.

The schools and neighborhoods closest to my childhood home were multi-cultural. I grew up near both San Francisco and New York City, where I had opportunities to experience that America is a "melting pot" of races and ethnicities. The Sunday morning service at Blessed International Church was a special one for me. I was a blue-eyed Caucasian minority among dark-eyed, dark-haired Korean Americans. Well, except for Janet, whose hair I remember was a lovely shade of black with royal blue highlights at the time. Thankfully their Sunday service was in English, because I had not started taking Korean lessons yet.

Church members and elders knew I was coming to visit. They were welcoming and also seemed encouraged. I was happy I could bring them some confirmation of their decision to send one of their daughters as their first missionary to Hongdae in Seoul, South Korea. When I met Elder Gloria, she said to me, you are a "Mother of Asia." She was the first person to speak that title to me. I did not know what she meant. Gloria said I would also be going to other countries. A bigger picture started to appear. It was more than my mind and heart could fully develop.

32.
FINDING MORE CLUES

In 2015, I found more clues on my path. Daily walks were more than outdoor exercise. They became treasure hunts, with my eyes scanning the ground, looking for more clues. I walked twenty minutes upriver and twenty minutes back. Each item I found was close to the spot where I had found the Asian coin.

The next item I found lying on the path was a page out of the children's storybook Cinderella. The picture showed Cinderella's elegant coach. As I picked it up, I heard the words, "Your prince has come." One of the Korean entertainers I prayed for was Jang Keun Suk, whose nickname was the "Prince of Asia." I also prayed for the actress/model, Park Shin Hye, who starred in the music video "Cinderella," which was also the name of a song recorded by the band CNBLUE, whose four members I prayed for daily. Finding the page was a confirmation to me that I was praying for the right Korean entertainers.

Weeks later, I found a colorful wrapper lying in the middle of the path. It was about the size of one from a pack of baseball cards. It had a cartoon drawing of an Asian male sitting behind a steering wheel with a stressed look on his face. Seoul is known for its nice automobiles. The entertainers like to drive expensive luxury cars.

I read an article about Jang Keun Suk having an accident in his Porsche. I felt an urgency to pray for the driving safety of the young Korean entertainers on my prayer list.

The next time I went to the local Japanese restaurant, I asked the owner at the counter if she could read the wrapper for me. She looked surprised and asked, "Where did you find this?" She explained it was from a Japanese toy and was designed to look like a travel poster. It said, "If you're sleepy when you're driving, be careful to be safe." I was encouraged to learn that I had prayed correctly. My daily exercise was fast becoming a treasure-hunting adventure.

During those months, I walked many miles on my path as I prayed for Korea. I prayed for the destiny of the younger generation, wisdom and integrity for governmental leaders, hope for the depressed, and protection for those in mental anguish. I learned that the citizens who chose the corporate path with successful companies were valued more highly than were the creative people among their culture. The artists, musicians, and actors in Korea's entertainment industry became a primary focus of my prayer time. I have always enjoyed being a creative in this world and having talented friends in the artistic community.

On a day trip to the Oregon coast, I enjoyed walking along historic Nye Beach. It was the same stretch of beach I had walked on several Mother's Days, as I lamented not having a child. As I looked across the Pacific Ocean in the direction of Korea, my heart felt wonderfully warmed. I felt my prayers were joining with those of many others spoken through the years on Korea's behalf.

Korean Christians are mighty prayer warriors as is evidenced by a place near Seoul called "Prayer Mountain." Established in 1978, it provided a secluded place for worship and prayer. Tiny one-person rooms are available for private prayer and overnight stays. The rooms were simple, furnished with a light, a desk, and a small bed. Shoes left outside the doors indicated which rooms were occupied. On a stroll about the property, people have reported hearing the travail of fervent prayer warriors rising from the mountain.

My humble prayers prepared my heart for my Korean adventure. One day I heard the spirit say, "It's Korea's time."

Then you will call upon me and come and pray to me,
and I will listen to you.
— Jeremiah 29:12

As I prayed for Korea, I often pictured the male I saw in my vision standing on a street corner in Seoul wearing his burgundy sweater. Though I believed I would meet him on my trip, he was still just a vision, a man with no name. To me, he symbolized the artistic ones I felt compassion toward and had been praying for. He was an unknown person I had yet to meet. Even though he lived thousands of miles away, in faith I prayed for him. I later learned that I was led to pray just when he was questioning his life, needed encouragement, and was seeking direction. The cry of this man's heart was heard.

You did not choose Me, but I chose you, and appointed you
that you might go and bear fruit, fruit that will last—and so that
whatever you ask in my name the Father will give you.
— John 15:16

33.
MAKING KOREAN
CONNECTIONS

When I met Pastors Ryan, Joanne, and Janet of Blessed International Church in May, I learned that they were sending a team to Seoul in early October of 2016. Since I had been expecting to go to Korea in October, I was confident they were the team I was to join with, so I made my Oregon-to-Korea airline reservations.

In the meantime, I was invited to attend a fan-club luncheon for the singer, model, actor, and director Jang Keun Suk, by Chris, a staff member at his Tree J Company. I had prayed for the young entertainer for almost a year. I felt so confident that I should accept her invitation that I spent $250 to change my airline reservation to arrive a few days earlier. Keun Suk was the K-Drama actor that first caught my attention and sparked my interest in Korea's arts and entertainment industry. Unfortunately, when Chris learned I was not an Official JKS Fan Club member, I was not allowed to go to the luncheon. When she did enroll me as an official member, all the reservations had already been booked.

I was disappointed that I could not go to the luncheon and possibly meet the actor I had been praying for, but I trusted there was a reason why I would arrive in Seoul four days ahead of my Southern California team members. Chris graciously invited me to join her for lunch when I arrived. I had said, "Yes" to my Korean adventure, and many extraordinary things had already taken place. It was no time to begin doubting whether everything was perfectly timed for me. I assumed there would be some surprises during my first few days in Korea.

The city of Seoul has a population of ten million people; including the surrounding area, there are twenty-two million people. After only eight Korean lessons with Young Eun Lee, my Oregon teacher, I knew only a few basic words and phrases and how to handle Korean money. When I saw the map of Seoul's massive subway system, it looked complex. I would travel by myself from Portland, Oregon, through Seattle, Washington, to the world-class Incheon International Airport in South Korea. I knew that entering Korea would be a "WOW" experience.

Years earlier, my friend Marty had told me about a young businessman she thought I should meet. Her sons had gone to an Oregon university with Shawn. She explained that he was an entrepreneur like I was and that he also loved Oregon. Trusting her discernment, I connected with him on Facebook. Shawn invited me to join him and his wife Mint for lunch and sightseeing on my first day in Korea. He posted photographs on Facebook of a lovely downtown hotel that looked like the kind of place in the city-center I had envisioned staying. Months before my trip, while praying for Seoul, I saw myself looking out an upper-floor window in a downtown hotel. Shawn's friend managed the new hotel, and he helped me make reservations. It was comforting to know that I would meet Shawn and Mint on my first day and share a meal and tour of Seoul. I appreciated my Oregon friends connecting me with my new Korean friends.

There is a "peace that passes understanding." Step by step, I felt led by that peace. A vision was given. I found my Korea team. October plane tickets were purchased. A nice hotel room was reserved. An itinerary and strategic plans came during my prayer times. One detail at a time, things lined up. All I had seen helped me to trust for what I did not yet see. As American architect Frank Lloyd Wright said, "God is in the details."

And the peace of God which transcends all understanding,
will guard your hearts and minds in Christ Jesus.
— Philippians 4:7

My team would arrive a few days after me. I planned to rest and venture out on my own during the day. The hotel's amenities promised a generous breakfast buffet with Western food choices, spacious lounges, and well-appointed rooms. Being an "urban missionary" would definitely have its benefits, but I knew I was sure to experience some unique challenges, too.

In comparison, I took an adventurous mission trip to Africa in 2008 that provided me with both challenges and rich blessings. While in Uganda, "The Pearl of Africa," our team was encouraged to continually say, "This is Africa" to remind ourselves that we were in a primitive country and that there were many things we could not change. In Uganda, we carefully navigated food choices and avoided drinking the water or anything washed in it. As careful as we were, team members took turns being sick. When Western toilets were unavailable, women peed standing over a six-inch hole — it was a hit-or-miss experience. I came away from Africa thinking that everyone in America should spend time there and experience that loving impoverished people does make a difference. I was thankful that Korea provided me indoor plumbing and modern amenities.

I am an experienced traveler who has booked reservations, navigated airports, and traveled all my life. However, the thought of entering Korea's dense population and not speaking the language fluently caused insecurity. I prayed that someone could meet me at the airport, help me exchange money, and guide me to my hotel. A few months before I was scheduled to go, my long-time friend, Larry, from New Zealand, texted me on Facebook and asked how I was doing. I told him I was going to South Korea. He said, "If you're going to Seoul, you need to meet my friend, Jinho." "Who is Jinho?" I asked. He said they were Facebook friends through a fan group of American jazz guitarist Pat Metheny. Trusting Larry's recommendation, I asked if he thought Jinho would meet me at the airport and help me get to my city-center hotel. Larry thought he would and added, "He's a really nice guy." I hoped that Jinho might be the answer to my prayers.

> *"Music makes the world go around and*
> *connects hearts and destinies."*
> *— Linda Dodson*

I looked at Jinho's Facebook page. You can learn a little about someone from the photographs and writings they post. I discovered that Jinho was a musician, which was of interest to me since I had been praying for Korea's artists, musicians, and entertainers. Our team was also focused on Hongdae, one of the creative districts in Seoul where there were many clubs and street performers. I began to imagine the discussions I could have with Jinho about music and the arts in Korea. While reading some of his posts and seeing his responses to his Facebook "friends," I could tell he was a warm, kind person. I felt peaceful about contacting him, and so did my husband, Tim.

Larry also wrote Jinho and encouraged him to help me — again, a friend in New Zealand helped a friend in the United States make a good connection in Korea. Living in the age of Internet technology is certainly a benefit for a modern-day missionary. I wrote Jinho a note on Facebook. Shortly after that, he responded by saying he could meet me at the airport and help me. He later told me that he also looked at my Facebook page and thought I seemed like a nice lady. I learned that, since Jinho was in junior high school, he looked for English-speaking tourists to help so he could practice speaking English with them. He hoped maybe I could help him with his English, too. I was relieved to know that Jinho would meet me when I arrived in Korea.

I wanted to bring a few gifts to people in Korea. I prayed about what to buy. While shopping one day, I felt strongly that I should buy a nice watch, but I knew that the style of watch one wears is a matter of personal taste. I also learned that many Koreans had expensive tastes and preferred name brands. My budget was limited, however, in the designer-watch category. I considered various brands and finally decided on the popular, sporty Fitbit watch. A sales assistant at the Target department store seemed to be a Fitbit expert and knew that the hottest-selling watch among males was one with a black band.

The Fitbit watch face was large, and its band was wide. I questioned the choice because I thought it might look too big on the typical medium-sized Korean man. But feeling sure it was the watch I was supposed to buy, I made my purchase. During prayer, I also remembered hearing the words, "It's Korea's time!" A watch certainly fit that declaration. The Fitbit watch was the most expensive gift that I purchased for my trip and I did not even know whom it was for. My adventure continued.

34.
PREPARING FOR
MY FAITH JOURNEY

In the months leading up to our Korea trip, our seven-woman team had monthly Skype calls. It was fun connecting face to face as we envisioned, prayed, and laughed together. As we met, the uncharted territory of our mission began to be defined, like strategic plans being rolled out in a military briefing. Our personalities blended well, and the team dynamics were good. It was an awesome, larger-than-me feeling to be part of a plan that I watched being divinely orchestrated.

As my departure date approached, I became more and more expectant. From the moment I first found the shiny Asian coin on my path, I sensed something amazing was taking place. What happened was definitely beyond my ability to ask for, imagine, or plan.

> *And without faith, it's impossible to please God,*
> *because anyone who comes to him must believe*
> *that he exists and that he rewards those who*
> *earnestly seek him.*
> *— Hebrews 11:6*

For months, I walked toward an adventure that was in the distant future. Sometimes I could see just far enough ahead to take my next step. I often wanted to know more details, but I was on a faith adventure that required patience as my plans gradually developed.

I remained committed to going with the flow and following my Leader. I was thankful I had the faith to trust that I was being called to Korea. That is how a missionary is required to go — by faith, willingly, and humbly. I continued taking baby steps. I searched for and found my team. I bought airplane tickets. I continued to seek guidance and pray. I believed in the vision and kept moving toward it. I knew I'd been called to my mission, but I had to push through feelings of inadequacy. I did not speak Korean, and my lessons were not progressing as quickly as I had hoped, even though my sweet teacher, Young Eun, encouraged me when she said I was her best student. Korean is a challenging language to learn, and their alphabet consists of symbols instead of letters. Once I got to Korea and heard conversations moving rapidly around me, I realized my communication skills were definitely deficient, despite my efforts to learn the language in only eight lessons.

In Korea, I relied heavily on smiling and saying "Hello" (여보세요) and "Thank you" (고맙습니다) as I made a polite bow. I was unfamiliar with Korean customs, and there were many. Their culture has a hierarchical structure of acceptable, informal-to-formal language, and proper protocol that I needed to know and follow.

"God doesn't call the qualified; he qualifies the called."
— Mark Batterson, Pastor
National Community Church
Washington, DC

I learned that in Korea, people are judged largely on their intelligence, appearance, credentials, and financial status. Men are the dominant gender and are respected more highly than the women are. The young are more esteemed than the elderly. The handsome and beautiful are more admired than are the average and simple. As a Christian, I am not a Biblical scholar or the graduate of a theological seminary. By Korean standards, I thought I might not appear impressive or successful in their eyes. I realized I needed to see myself as He sees me and not be intimidated by the opinions or judgments of those I was about to meet.

I smiled as I asked, "Really — I was chosen for this mission?" The bottom line was this: I had what I needed most: "…Christ in me, the hope of glory." (Colossians 1:27) I could not allow myself to be held back by the belief that, somehow, I was not enough. My calling to Korea was not about proving that I was adequate, strong, or perfect. My age was also not relevant in the kingdom of God, but my passion, willingness, and obedience were. As I removed the self-restraint on my own thinking, I was free to imagine future possibilities that existed outside the limitations of my own thinking. To those of you who are not part of the younger generation, I can now confidently say from my own experience, that some of your best days may still be ahead of you. It does not matter if you are twenty or past sixty. It is not too late for wonderful, unexpected things to happen in your life. You can still make significant contributions. I trusted that whatever I needed would be provided. This truth also encouraged me:

But God chose the foolish things of the world to shame the wise;
God chose the weak things of the world to shame the strong.
God chose the lowly things of this world and the despised things…
so that no one may boast before him.
— 1 Corinthians 1:27-29

Having a genuine love for Korea and the people I was being sent to was what I needed most. I trusted that His love for me and in me was unfailing. I knew that "I can do all things through Christ who strengthens me." (Philippians 4:13) My mission would be successful because He lived in me and would flow through me to bless others. I was encouraged as I watched all the details of my Korea trip being confirmed and the puzzle pieces gradually sliding into place.

I am thankful for His still, small voice. He spoke in analogies, parables, and through His Word. He communicated with me through visual images and in simple life moments. I saw with the eyes of my spirit in daydreams and night visions. He spoke through the people around me when I sought their discernment and asked for their prayers. I valued the wisdom of those who loved Him and who loved me.

Throughout the weeks and months of 2015-2016, I filled the pages in my journals with the impressions I thought should be recorded. Many people have asked, "How do I know God's will?" I found a good article on the web by Pastor Robert Morris, of the Gateway Church in Dallas, Texas, titled: "10 Powerful Ways God Speaks in the Bible." He said, "It is vital that we see not only that God speaks, but also how he speaks."

He Speaks in These Powerful Ways

- Through circumstances   Jonah 1-4
- Through wise counsel   Proverbs — all
- Through peace   Colossians 3:15
- Through people   Seen throughout the Bible.
- Through dreams and visions   Acts 2:17, Joel 2:28
- Through our thoughts   Amos 4:13, Matthew 1:19-21
- Through natural manifestations   John 12:27-30, Acts 9:1-15
- Through supernatural manifestations   Exodus 3:1-4, Judges 6:37-40
                                        Acts 9:1-15, Numbers 22:1-35
- Through the Bible   2 Timothy 3:16, Hebrews 4:12
- Through a whisper   1 Kings 19:12

In his article, Pastor Morris expressed the importance of hearing. And once we did, we needed to act in faith. "Have you heard and truly listened to His voice? Then, good — now is the time to move with confidence," Robert encouraged.

I Love Journaling

Through the years, I learned the importance of capturing inspired thoughts and pictures in a purse-sized journal that I carried with me. I believed that some ideas were worthy of being recorded in a permanent place. Otherwise, those impressions could have faded with time and been lost forever. When I could not write, I often voice-recorded thoughts on my iPhone to be transcribed later. After I filled up a journal, I enjoyed reading the pages from front to back as I reflected on the thoughts that came during my quiet times. Writing brought me joy. I made it a personal goal to be a faithful scribe.

As my Korea trip approached, my commitment to the mission was tested. Many times, I was asked, "Will you keep saying 'Yes' to my invitation?" I had experienced too many obvious blessings to question the opportunity being offered to me. As I have reread my journals from that time, my faith has continued to be encouraged. I like feeling that I passed my faith tests.

Prophetic Word for Korea

Just today, I found a prophetic word I had recorded in August of 2015, two months before I went to Korea:

"I am sending a company of people to Korea whom I can trust. You are mine, and I am yours. Ask whatever you wish in my name, and it shall be done for you. My hosts of heaven are ready and waiting to be dispatched on a moment's notice. They will go before you to clear the way for my power and my glory to flow from you.

"You are a well. You are a well of my glory. There has never been a time like this time in all of history. The nations are opening to my people. You will be a people able to hear, see, and do like never before. I am the God of the exceedingly and abundantly beyond all you can ask or imagine. This is not a time for the timid. This is a time for the warrior bride who can take the land and see great deliverance for those in bondage.

"Many before you longed to see what you will see open up for you. Now is the time for deliverance and for freedom in the Spirit to gain great victories. Trust your paths to my Holy Spirit, who is your faithful guide. You are mine; never doubt that. Place your

confidence not in the arm of the flesh, but wholly in me. I will set your cadence. Your feet are shod with the Gospel of peace. You are clothed in my righteousness. You are mine."

SCENE 7:
THE "GO YEARS"

*Take delight in the Lord and he will give you
the desires of your heart.*
— Psalm 37:4

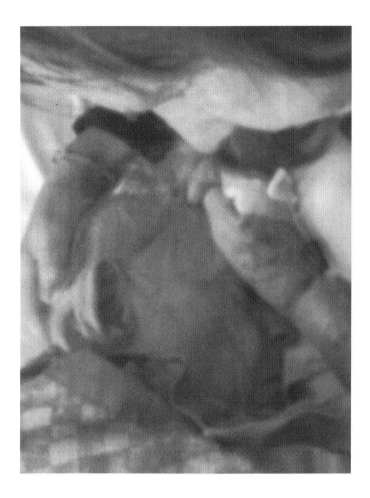

35.
MY MOTHER'S
CHALLENGING SEASON

When my mother moved from Ohio to Oregon in 2009 to be close to her children and grandchildren, my responsibilities as oldest daughter increased. It was my time to help parents finish well. I had not lived with my mom and dad since I left home at nineteen years old. There were many times that I missed my mother. During "Mom's Weekend" at OSU or at special events in my life, I wished she were there. When I felt alone or insecure, I wanted my mom to ask me her good questions and offer motherly advice. On Mother's Day and her birthday, I just wanted her there so I could celebrate her being my mom.

In my big home country of America, people are commonly separated from one another. We primarily move for the right opportunity, affordable housing, and living near those who matter most. Some us have lived in different states, many miles from our families. I have not lived in the idealistic Norman Rockwell world, where my loved ones are just down a tree-lined street and around the corner from one another. After years of being separated by miles, it was my joy to have my mom in Oregon to share family events and mother-daughter time.

For sixty years, Mom had been married and never lived alone. She was an extroverted "people person" who got lonely by herself.

When Paul met mom at the senior center, he was quick to ask for her telephone number. Even in their eighties and nineties, they felt a spark and soon decided to marry. Family and friends gathered for Mary Lou and Paul's golden-years wedding. Sadly, Paul passed away only nine months later. After his cancer diagnosis, her precious husband died only just two short weeks later. Theirs was a sweet-but-too-short love story.

Mom and I planned regular dates and enjoyed spending time together. Unfortunately, she began to experience a physical and mental decline, and our happy times quickly turned to challenging times. My mother, who had always considered herself "capable," was frightened by her own deterioration. Neither of us expected to deal with that kind of traumatic life experience.

When mom talked one day about possibly moving to Stonybrook, a gracious senior-living community, my siblings and I supported the idea and got her relocated there. She had her own spacious apartment and a lovely dining room where healthy meals were served. There were activities to enjoy and people to meet. Mom always had a talent for remembering the names and details of those around her. She was happiest among family and friends. I was relieved to know that mom was in a lovely, safe place, surrounded by people.

A new excitement entered mom's life when she met Pete at a community dance. Unfortunately, their relationship ended when he recognized the signs of her mental decline. His late wife had also suffered from dementia. Mom began having difficulty with routine tasks and reading the clock. I was sad to learn that a staff member found mom sitting in the unheated foyer early one morning feeling cold and confused. She had gotten confused about the time and waited all night for her ride to church to come.

Once a "social butterfly," mom withdrew from others into a lonely, fearful place. One of her nicknames was "Twenty Questions." She had been a professional interviewer of people, especially our prospective boyfriends and girlfriends, and asked her twenty (or more) questions. I was shocked to hear her struggling with words and have difficulty remembering names. When her condition worsened, we moved her again to an assisted-living facility, where loving caregivers could help her with medications and housekeeping tasks.

In mom's new "home" close to her family, her paranoia increased. Despite our constant reassurance, she felt anxious and insisted that someone was stealing her money and jewelry at night — a common fear among the fragile elderly. We found her valuables hidden in the trashcan, under her bed, and sandwiched between other items in her drawers. When she became a disruption to the other residents, we had to move mom again, this time to a smaller, adult foster home with only five residents. It was such an emotional time for us all, especially my dear mom.

In many ways, she became like my child and I her mother, not the kind of mother I had ever expected or wanted to be. One day when I was sitting with mom, holding her hand, she thanked me for taking good care of her. "You're welcome, Mom," I responded. Then I asked her, "Mom, who is going to take care of me when I get old?" She sweetly and confidently replied, "Oh, I will, honey." At that point, she was obviously not aware of how quickly she was changing. Nevertheless, I felt touched that she planned to be there for me when I was old.

As mom rapidly declined, we went to a neurologist who observed and tested her. Due to the deterioration of her language, she was diagnosed with "Advanced Alzheimer's disease." Her memory loss and decreased communication were difficult for us all, especially for mom. As her abilities diminished, I watched her agony and sorrow increase. She became more teary, agitated, and fearful. One day she looked at me and clearly said, "Let's get out of here!" And believe me, I sure wanted to rescue her from her downward spiral.

Mom had been active throughout her life. She was on the winning debate team in high school, handled the family finances, and was a capable, supportive woman. She kept a beautiful home and raised us well. She was the Chairman and President of numerous boards and organizations — just to name a few of her many talents. As she changed, there were so many things mom could not do. It was difficult to find the best medications and dosages for her. The drugs prescribed to ease her paranoia and sadness caused side effects and brought more confusion. At other times, she was overmedicated and became almost catatonic. When others said she could live like that for years, I pleaded for mercy. I did not want her to endure the dreadful disease for long, and I treasured every coherent moment with her.

Mom always remembered who I was, which I was thankful for. When I went to visit, she was always happy to see me. With brightness in her voice, she would say, "Linda!" But before our visit was over, she often started crying, due to an unknown cause. On her eighty-ninth birthday, I wanted to create happy moments for her. I brought refreshments for the residents and staff. My brother and his wife played guitar and sang. Her granddaughter and son-in-law also came to visit. The florist delivered a pretty sunflower bouquet from my sister that brought a smile to her face. Our little party had all the ingredients of a happy time, but mom began crying before we were even out the door. On the inside, I cried, too.

Many times, I prayed that mom would be of sound mind. Oh, how I prayed, as she slipped away from us, a few precious brain cells at a time. As the quality of her life declined, I realized all I could really do was to love her and hope for some good moments. Though her finale was difficult, I was thankful for the opportunities I had to love her. I also appreciated the friends and family members who visited mom and supported us through a challenging time.

As my October trip to Korea drew near, I sensed that something was going to happen to mom around the time of my departure. The day before I was leaving for Korea, I got a phone call from her caregiver, who told me that mom had fallen and was in an ambulance, on her way to the emergency room. While she was sitting in her wheelchair, mom had tried to get over a raised place on the floor, and she scooted herself right out of her seat. Her butt dropped just one foot and hit the floor. They told me she was in severe pain. When I received the call, I was just packing my suitcase for Korea. I had planned to see mom one more time on my way to the airport hotel.

I rushed out the door for the hospital and arrived at the emergency-room entrance just as mom's ambulance was arriving. When they opened the ambulance doors, my face was the first one she saw. She heard my voice — "Hi, Mom. I'm here" — and she opened her pained eyes in response. She could not speak but communicated through her moaning. They had given her a big dose of morphine, but she was still feeling severe pain. Mom had always been fairly pain-tolerant, but her facial expressions and groans told me she was hurting badly. I feared that she had broken her hip. In the emergency room, I whispered in her ear, "Mom, they are going to take some x-rays, and, if something is broken, we will get it fixed." In the sweetest voice imaginable, she said, "Thank you." Her warm response touched my heart.

The x-ray report was not good. Even though mom had dropped only a short distance to the floor, the images showed she had broken her hip in three places, and the ball joint was completely severed.

Her condition was serious; she was eighty-nine years of age, and I was not sure they could even put her back together again. During my consultation with the surgeon, he explained they would try to reattach the broken pieces of mom's hip. His goals were basic: put her hip back together, minimize her pain, and hopefully extend her life. I knew that a traumatic event and major surgery could push mom deeper into Alzheimer's disease. Change, trauma, and anesthesia are known for increasing the symptoms of dementia. I knew that she might not even survive a major surgery. Oh, my precious mommy! My daughter's heart ached for her.

Song: *"Blank Stares," by Jay Allen*

36.
CALLED TO GO

To say that I questioned my travel plans to Korea would be an understatement. "Should I still go?" I asked my husband. "Absolutely," he responded. My brother added, "Yes, definitely. You are called." Without their reassurance, I am not sure I could have gone. When Mom moved to Oregon, I became her "go-to girl." I was the one most available to watch over her. I was her advocate at medical appointments and with care-facility staff. The thought of mom having surgery without me being there was difficult.

When mom got more medication for her intense pain, she became unconscious, and I could not communicate with her at all. There could be no final words or "goodbyes." As she lay curled up in her pain, I leaned over my mom and gave her my last kisses. I had the feeling I would not see her again in this lifetime, though I did pray for a successful surgery. I had to trust that God would take care of my sweet mommy.

A male nurse came to wheel mom's bed to the operating room. I told him that, if anything should happen and she did not survive the surgery, I wanted the team to know that she had lived a good life. I knew the surgery was risky, and I wanted to offer him some comfort in that moment. I was alone, and I needed someone to comfort ME in that moment! When I told the nurse that I was leaving for Korea, he got a serious look on his face. Then he said to me — in Korean — "Thank you (고맙습니다)." That was a Korean word I did know. I asked him, "How do you know Korean?" He explained that he and his wife had lived there for a few years.

I wondered, "What are the odds that a male nurse, who lived in Korea, would come to get my mom for surgery and thank me in Korean?" I felt like God himself was thanking me for my willingness to go. It was a deeply personal moment for me. As emotionally tough as it was to leave my precious mom, I knew I must. I stood alone in the hallway, watching her being rolled away to surgery. As the elevator doors closed, cutting off my view of her, tears rolled down my cheeks. I remembered that I had sensed some event would occur with mom around the time of my departure for Korea. I was prepared in advance for that emotional day. He knew it was coming; being reminded of that brought me some comfort.

I took a tearful walk to my car. My daughter's heart wanted to turn back to be with my mommy. I had always walked toward her in her time of need, not away from her. That afternoon, however, it was confirmed three times that I should go to Korea. It was an emotional decision. As I was driving home to get my suitcase, this scripture came to my mind:

Anyone who loves father or mother
more than me, is not worthy of me.
Anyone who loves son or daughter
more than me, is not worthy of me.
Anyone who does not take up his cross
and follow me, is not worthy of me.
—Matthew 10:37-38

In His gentle, loving voice, I heard Him whisper, "Linda, you are worthy of me."

On a walk in the full moon one October evening in 2017, my friend and I listened to Italian composer Ennio Morricone's film score from the inspiring motion picture The Mission. That day marked the one-year anniversary of my mom's death. As we listened to the beautiful music, I remembered how I felt as I left the hospital knowing I would not be there to hold my mom's hand, bring her flowers or a Wendy's frosty, or pray for her. Healing tears flowed as I re-experienced my loss of her.

In the past, I had been there to care for mom, to be her communicator, or to rub lotion on her hands and arms. I could usually put a smile on her face and calm her with my words or simply my presence. When I went to Korea, I had to leave her in the care of other family members and a doctor we did not know. I stepped out of my oldest-daughter responsibilities and into my new role as an urban missionary to Korea. There is often a requirement that is difficult to meet, a price that must be paid. Before you build, or say, "Yes," or you "Go into all the world," do pause and consider the cost.

Suppose one of you wants to build a tower. Won't you first sit down and estimate the cost to see if you have enough money to complete it? For if you lay the foundation and are not able to finish it, everyone who sees it will ridicule you, saying, "This person began to build and wasn't able to finish."
— Luke 14:28-30

On my drive to the airport hotel and in bed that night, I considered the cost. On my long flight to Korea, I prayed for mom and wondered, How will I be judged by the Koreans I am about to meet? Honoring elders is expected in the Korean culture. Would they think I was a dishonorable daughter who had abandoned my mother in her time of need? At that point, I could only trust God with the matter. Sometimes we get to stay with family, and, at other times, we must leave them and go where we are called.

On my way to Korea, I received the happy news that the surgeon had been able to reconnect the broken pieces of mom's hip and that her pain had lessened greatly. Within a couple of days, she returned to her loving care home and was able to sit in her wheelchair and stand. I was concerned about whether mom's mind would fully recover from the anesthesia and major surgery, but I was relieved and thankful to hear good reports from home. I looked forward to sharing stories from my trip with mom and was hopeful she could at least enjoy seeing my photographs.

My prayers for mom's successful surgery were answered. I had kept my promise to her that, if something was broken, we would get it fixed. The good news about mom brought me the relief I needed to step into my Korean adventure.

Like cold water to a weary soul
is good news from a distant land.
— Proverbs 25:25

Song: *"The Mission," by Ennio Morricone*

37.
MAIDEN VOYAGE
TO KOREA

As my plane landed at Korea's Incheon International Airport, my heart started to beat a little faster. The sign on the exit ramp made it real: "Welcome to South Korea." I entered my Asian adventure surrounded by beautiful, black-haired, dark-eyed people speaking Korean. I was suddenly a blue-eyed minority in a new country. At the first immigration checkpoint, a lovely young female hostess wearing a colorful hanbok (traditional Korean dress) welcomed us weary travelers.

I successfully maneuvered my luggage and got through the first passport-inspection station. Then I texted Jinho to let him know I had arrived. I said he could recognize me as the lady wearing the red beret. Tim had asked me to take a picture with Jinho so he would know I arrived there safely. It was a comfort to receive Jinho's response saying he was waiting just outside the secure area. I had butterflies swirling in my tummy. I felt weary from my 6,000-mile journey, but my excitement provided the rush of adrenaline I needed to connect with my new friend.

When I came through the doors, Jinho recognized me and greeted me with a big smile and a polite bow, as he lifted the heavy bag off my shoulders. That is the moment my "Wow Adventure" jump-started!

When I saw Jinho, I realized he was the man in the burgundy sweater I had seen in my vision six months before. It was reassuring to know that I was in the right place, at the right time, with the right person.

On our hour-long bus ride to downtown Seoul, I got my first glimpse of the Han River, the Mapo Bridge, and the lovely mountains that surrounded Seoul. The cityscape was an interesting blend of ancient history and modern architecture, and all the hustle-bustle of ten million people that I had imagined. It was comforting to have Jinho as my first travel guide. He shared many interesting things about his country. When I heard Koreans talking on the bus, I was relieved that Jinho's English skills were good, since my Korean was seriously lacking.

When we arrived at my Namdaemun Marriott Hotel, I invited Jinho to join me for dinner. He had traveled quite a distance to meet me at the airport and would get home late that night. I noticed a sign in the hotel lobby advertising their Friday-night seafood buffet, so we decided to eat there. The beautiful seafood display was abundant and offered familiar American foods and gorgeous king crab legs. My allergies demanded that I be careful with food choices in order to stay healthy. Not getting a migraine headache was a priority. I felt jet-lagged and was not synchronized with Korea time yet, so I was not very interested in food. I focused more on my enjoyable conversation with Jinho. I should have asked the cost of the buffet. When the bill came, it was $150. Oops!

During dinner, I thought about the Fitbit watch I had purchased and felt certain it was for Jinho. On the airplane, I had prayed and asked for a word of encouragement to give him and I heard, "Tell him: I make all things beautiful in my time" (from Ecclesiastes 3:11). It was a verse that fit well with my gift, so, after dinner, I gave Jinho the watch. When I bought the Fitbit, I was concerned that it might look too large on a medium-sized Korean man. But on six-foot-two-inch Jinho, it looked just right.

Jinho asked what my plans were for the next few days. I said I thought I would just relax at the hotel until my team arrived and venture out on my own during the day. He asked if I knew how to navigate the subway system. I told him the subway map looked quite complicated, and he agreed that it was. He kindly offered to show me some sights in Seoul. Since I had changed my airplane ticket to arrive earlier, I expected that more blessings were sure to come.

Days before I left for Korea, I had heard the worship song, "Oceans" by Hillsong UNITED. The lyrics beautifully expressed a deeper faith that was being stirred up in my own heart. I was being drawn out upon the waters, into the great unknown, where my feet may fail, and I would call upon His name. I was being asked to trust on a greater level than I ever had before. I was thankful for songwriters like Michael, Matt, Joel, and Salomon for their inspiring lyrics that encouraged me throughout my time in Korea. "Oceans" became my theme song on my first trip.

Song: "Oceans," by Hillsong featuring Taya Smith

38.
CARRIED BY PRAYER

My calling to "...go into all the world..." (Mark 16:15) would not have been possible without the prayers of those who loved me. Prayers birthed my original vision of Korea's Hongdae district. Prayer cultivated my heart so that Korea could be planted there. During prayer times, the details of my mission trip were revealed. Family and friends believed me when I told them I felt called to Korea, for purposes not fully realized, and they prayed for me. As I continued to pray, I received the courage to say "Yes" to my invitation. I was thankful for my prayer warriors, spiritual midwives, and those who loved me. Their prayers covered me. Loving prayers were, and still are, the wind beneath my wings.

This is one of my favorite prayer scriptures:

"For this reason, since the day we heard about you, we have not stopped praying for you. We continually ask God to fill you with the knowledge of his will through all the wisdom and understanding that the Spirit gives, so that you may live a life worthy of the Lord and please him in every way: bearing fruit in every good work, growing in the knowledge of God, being strengthened with all power according to

his glorious might so that you may have great endurance and patience,
and giving joyful thanks to the Father, who has qualified you to share
in the inheritance of his holy people in the kingdom of light."
— Colossians 1:9-12

My husband sent this e-mail to my prayer team:

"Hi, friends! Welcome to this private group that will be sharing Linda's Korean adventure, her first step in response to a call of God who has "put Asia on her path." October 6, she flew from PDX to SEA and then departed SEA for INC (Incheon International Airport) near Seoul, a twelve-hour flight. I will post her itinerary.

"Linda is part of a ministry trip with a group from Blessed International Church in Anaheim, CA. (That connection is an amazing story.) They will be ministering on the streets of Seoul, especially in the artistic and collegiate district of Hongdae. As they minister, they will be seeking God's guidance regarding the future establishment of an "equipping center" in Seoul to support other Christians in Korea. They will be looking for inspiration, guidance, and opportunities — this is an "exploratory trip."

"Linda will be 'on her own' Friday through Sunday, but in the care of a very interesting Korean, Jinho Choi, that she has been connected to by another friend in New Zealand we've known for many years; that is another amazing story. On Monday, she will join the rest of the team as they arrive in Seoul.

"Linda and the team will be very grateful for your prayers and words of encouragement. Please check this page periodically for news from Linda and to send your positive support.

Thank you!
Tim"

An encouraging text from my friend Marty:

"I'm praying this morning. Hopefully you are sleeping peacefully right now. I pray blessing on your reception, your health, your speaking Korean! I believe that every Korean you meet will encounter the love and beauty of God manifested through you, dear Linda. Everywhere you go, the atmosphere will be charged with the presence of God. You were made for this adventure. You go, mother of Asia. We are so proud of you."

A prayer from Catherine:

"May the Lord remain constantly at your side and his mercy guide your journey in ways that are pleasing to Him. May God bless you, Linda, with every heavenly blessing and give you a safe journey; wherever life leads you may you find Him there to protect you. Safe Journey, Blessings, Catherine, your friend in Christ."

39.
MY "WOW! JOURNEY"

South Korea, 2016

My three-week "WOW! Journey" was super. I captured some daily highlights from my journal so you can share in the joy of my trip to South Korea. The vision was birthed!

What a full, adventurous trip it was. I was often on the go, walking among the crowds, climbing up and down stairways, riding in cabs, dining in restaurants, rushing onto crammed subways, and encountering divine appointments. Days were long, and most nights were short. As I traveled on highways and in trains, I journeyed deeper into His heart. I prayed through sleepless hours and landed on my knees on behalf of a nation and a people I grew to love more deeply.

My "Yes" took me to places I had never imagined going. I encountered new faces and more graces than I had previously known. There were times I felt on the edge of being overwhelmed, unsure if my physical body or emotions could handle more of His goodness. My journey was incredible. I experienced the truth of this promise:

My grace is sufficient for you.
My power is made perfect in weakness.
— 2 Corinthians 12:9

When I considered what I would have missed had I not gone to Korea, I was thankful for the inspiration, courage, and confirmations I received. Without Him, there would have been no journey, and my stories could not be told. My calling and my trip to Korea paved the way for future trips to the nations. I felt grateful and more confident in my ability to be led by Him. I am still in awe of it all!

Reflection: What are you feeling inspired to do? May you have prayer warriors and loved ones who will champion what you are called to for such a time as this.

Song: "Wind Beneath My Wings," by Bette Midler

...go into all the world and
preach the Gospel to all creation.
— Mark 16:15

Song: "Great Are You, Lord," by Casting Crowns

SCENE 8:
HE IS FAITHFUL

But you, Lord, are a compassionate and gracious God,
slow to anger, abounding in love and faithfulness.
— *Psalm 86:15*

40.
LETTERS FROM KOREA:
"DEAR PRAYER WARRIORS"

The following e-mail messages were written to those praying for me while I was in South Korea. They were the days when the prophecy I received, "I am putting Asia on your path," was fulfilled. I hope you enjoy sharing some memorable moments from my adventurous trip.

October 7 — Saturday night: My introduction to Seoul with Shawn and Mint

What a fun first day I had with my new Korean friends, Shawn and Mint. Our first stop was Insadong, a lovely district in Seoul, South Korea's capital. The parkway was lined with traditional gift shops and galleries. Lively groups of teenagers dressed in hanbok, traditional Korean clothing, added a youthful enthusiasm and an historic touch to an otherwise more-modern Seoul. I loved being out among the Korean people today. As we walked around, I was reminded of the following verse. I prayed boldly for His kingdom to come and His will to be done in Korea.

I will give you every place where you set your foot...
— Joshua 1:3

We shared a delicious lunch at one of Shawn's favorite traditional Korean restaurants, with its wood-beamed ceiling and small BBQ tables. I enjoyed getting to know a special Korean couple. After lunch, we walked to a charming, traditional teahouse for lemongrass tea and green tea milkshakes. The day's final treat was a drive to the Bugak Skyway along the northeast ridge of Bugaksan Mountain. It is one of Seoul's most scenic routes and a great place to enjoy wide, panoramic views of the city with a population of ten million. My hosts, Shawn and Mint, were gracious and kind.

I learned today that Seoul, South Korea, is seventy percent mountainous. In times of war, the natural geography protected the city from its invaders. The beauty of the surrounding mountains offered us a restful contrast to Seoul's otherwise very densely populated cityscape. It is filled with buildings, highways, and the Han River and its twenty-seven bridges, which provided scenic relief and accessibility to various areas of the city. What a wonderful, welcoming day I had in Seoul.

October 9, 2016: Finding my needle in the haystack

Even though today started with a debilitating migraine headache, it was special. I bravely explored the Namdaemun outdoor market across the street from my hotel by myself. It is the largest traditional market in Seoul and opened in 1964. It consisted of a maze of narrow alleyways between small shops, where the aroma of food carts and colorful, open-air booths delighted my senses. I purchased a few items and even negotiated prices. I practiced my limited Korean as I talked with the shop owners. There were many people out and about in this densely populated city and other American tourists to talk to.

My new Korean friend, Jinho, takes an hour-long subway ride to come be my tour guide. He is a blessing. We visited an English-speaking church where we both felt inspired. The pastor preached a message from the book of Esther that resonated with my spirit. I have definitely felt like an Esther on my mission.

> *…And who knows but that you have come to your*
> *royal position for such a time as this?*
> *— Esther 4:14*

After the service, we rode the bus to Itaewon, a District in Seoul where people of many nationalities live. Needing to be careful with food today because of my headache, we chose a Mexican restaurant, with familiar foods. While we waited for our table, we cruised the energetic neighborhood and browsed in the shops. There are always tourists and locals out and about, shopping, eating, and gathering around street musicians. Itaewon was continuously buzzing with activity.

On our walk back to the restaurant, I heard singing on a distant street corner. I recognized the voice as that of Joseph Butso, a young man from Ohio that I had watched in a YouTube video performing on the streets of Seoul — an activity they call "busking." Jinho said my mouth dropped wide open when I heard Joseph singing. We ran across the street and confirmed it was the young man I had wanted to meet!

On August 18, 2016, Joseph won a singing contest on the Korean program I Can See Your Voice 3 on Mnet/TVN with his stunning performance of "Saldaga." (살다가). As my ministry partner Janet and I were watching Joseph's videos back in September, I said, "We need to meet that guy." A desire of my heart was fulfilled today. Finding my needle in a giant haystack was easy for God.

Reflection: Do you have a dream that seems too big? Have faith to believe it can be realized; dreams really do come true!

Joseph is a gifted worshipper and street performer who speaks and sings fluently in Korean. When he worships on the streets of Seoul, crowds gather around him. He is an effective communicator of God's love. He shines. I talked with Joseph and told him that I had wanted to meet him. I said, "God told me it's Korea's time," and he enthusiastically agreed, replying, "Amen, amen!" Between songs, we talked briefly and exchanged email addresses. I have continued to pray for Joseph.

Going to Namsan Tower

Tomorrow Jinho and I will ride the cable car up Namsan Mountain, the second highest point overlooking Seoul, to see the city views and the 774-foot Namsan tower, which is visible from my hotel window. It looks like a good place to pray over Seoul. We will visit the Kyung Bok Gung palace before taking the subway to Mapo-gu near Hongdae to meet Janet and the team arriving from Malaysia. Seoul's public-transportation systems are so good that many people do not need cars for their daily commutes. Our eight-woman ministry time begins tomorrow night. I am thankful to have had three days for sightseeing and rest. As I expected, my arrival time was perfectly orchestrated. I am adjusted to Korea time and feel ready for the next chapter of this adventure.

I have appreciated Jinho's support. He is teaching me about Korean culture and history and has gotten me to where I needed to be. I am in good hands.

Reflection: Where do you want the support of others in your life? And whom can you support?

October 9, 2016: Korea's Hangul Day

After months of visioning, praying, and preparing, I am really in Korea! This morning, as I was waking, I heard the unexpected sounds of drumbeats and horse hooves outside my hotel window. What a delight it was to look outside and see Koreans dressed in colorful Joseon Dynasty clothing riding horseback, waving flags, and beating traditional Korean drums ("buk, 북") as they passed my hotel. The triumphal sight felt wonderfully welcoming!

I learned that the parade marked the opening of Hangul Day. Every year on October 9, Koreans celebrate King Sejong of the Joseon Dynasty (1418 to 1450), who personally led scholars in the creation of the Korean alphabet, Hangul. I hurried downstairs to watch as the beautiful pageantry passed by.

October 10, 2016: Praying from Namsan Mountain

From my hotel room, I can see the lighted night view of Korea's Namsan Tower. Jinho said the locals do not visit the attraction much, but he thought we should go there. We rode a cable car up the mountain to see the impressive city views. He pointed out the different features: the numerous bridges on the Han River, financial district, university area of Hongdae, and the recently completed 123-floor Lotte World Tower, the highest building in Korea. Namsan Mountain was the ideal place to pray for the city. Months before I arrived, I had seen myself praying from a high place overlooking Seoul.

The highest heavens belong to the Lord,
but the earth he has given to mankind.
— Psalm 115:16

"Locks of Love"

A fun feature of the Namsan Tower site is the "Locks of Love." Thousands of colorful locks are attached to the fences, gates, planters, and stair railings. Couples write their names on the locks as a pledge to not break their bond of love. Since we did not have a lock to attach, Jinho suggested that we write our names on the top of a wall facing the Hongdae District. I wondered if we would return there someday and find our names. We had an intermittent FaceTime with Tim from the mountaintop. This was one of my personal favorite times in Korea. I knew that one of the main reasons I was sent to Korea was to pray. Thank you, Jinho, for taking me there. Mission accomplished.

Reflection: What city or nation do you feel called to pray for?

October 11, 2016: Being led to artist Song Jae In

Jinho was my tour guide through another inspiring day. We visited the lovely Gyeongbokgung, the main royal palace. Built in 1395, it is commonly referred to as the Northern Palace. It is the most beautiful and largest of Seoul's five palaces. The premises were destroyed by fire during the Imjin War (Japanese Invasions, 1592 to 1598). During the reign of King Gojong (1852 to 1919) all the buildings were beautifully restored. We also saw the gorgeous Changdeokgung (창덕궁), the lovely Joseon Dynasty building that sits in the middle of a pond filled with large carp. I loved seeing Korea's beautiful national treasures.

Our peaceful stroll among historic Korean sites and ancient architecture was fascinating. It was fun mingling with the Korean people, especially the teenagers wearing their hanbok clothing. People who dressed in traditional outfits received free entry to the cultural sites. I had my photograph taken with a group of Korean girls, then with some young boys. I felt an unusual familiarity with the young people, and they were responsive to me. I saw adults herding groups of adorable, young Korean children in traditional clothes. Before I left America, I'd told my friend, "I know what's going to happen, I'm going to see those cute Korean children and want to bring one home with me." I did not know then just how prophetic my words were when I spoke them.

While Jinho and I visited the palace, a Chinese couple asked if we would take their picture in front of the Main Throne Hall. Then they

captured our photo for us. I was pleased we recorded the moment. That was the day I first sensed that Jinho and I were a gift to one another, for purposes not yet fully known. If I had not gone to Korea, we would not have connected and been positioned to receive many blessings. My obedience definitely brought its rewards to both of us.

Seoul has many winding, narrow alleys — "metropolitan mazes," I called them — filled with colorful signs and small shops selling items like handmade rice papers, bamboo brushes, ginseng, stylish hats, and traditional hanbok clothing. In a small courtyard surrounded by traditional buildings, we noticed a lovely painting displayed in a window, featuring an Asian interpretation of Jesus. We entered the gallery and were warmly greeted by the talented artist, Song Jae In. As Jinho taught me about the symbolism in her beautiful traditional paintings, I felt God's pleasure in her work.

Song Jae In was among the group of Korean artists and entertainers I had been praying for before I left Oregon. With Jinho interpreting, we asked if we could pray for her. She enthusiastically welcomed our prayers. Song held my hand tightly in hers. As I prayed, I felt God's deep love for her. I envisioned her sitting at her easel with a big smile on her face as she received fresh inspiration for her paintings. I shared my vision with her. Song warmly expressed her appreciation and gave us a book of her lovely paintings and a small red-and-gold satin pouch filled with traditional cookies. Praying for people is one of my favorite things to do. I was thankful we were led to her today. I was on the lookout for "the one" to love. We had a sweet, memorable time with a talented artist. Our hearts were touched, and so was hers. There were no racial or cultural barriers in art and love.

Reflection: Pray that artists and musicians will receive the inspiration and support they need to continue creating. Our world needs the inspired art and music of the gifted ones!

Moving Into Hongdae

My Oregon friend and Korean adoptee, Kourtni, spent her final day in Seoul before she returned to the USA. She arranges trips for other adoptees to help connect them to their roots and possibly meet their birth parents. We had a fun rendezvous with her in Hongdae.

Before I arrived in Korea, I had seen photographs of the Hongdae area, where our team would be ministering. Today I literally walked into the vision I had been pregnant with for nine months. The 'pictures I saw online were inadequate preparation for my first visit. There was so much sensory input in Hongdae: flashing signs, loud music, noisy traffic, crowded little shops, and narrow streets packed with young people — it was like a mini-Vegas on steroids. I am no stranger to lively cities, but my entry into Hongdae was definitely an over-stimulating one.

> *Lift up your heads, you gates; be lifted up, you ancient doors,*
> *that the King of glory may come in.*
> *— Psalm 24:7*

When we arrived in Hongdae and I saw all the college students, I became deeply emotional. A part of me felt like I already knew them — like they were my kids. I had been praying for them months before I arrived. There was one tree-lined street in the middle of Hongdae where I felt His presence most intensely. In a grassy center strip on that street, there was a concrete sculpture of a king's throne. Half of the throne was well built, and half of it was purposely deteriorated. When I saw the throne, I heard the words, "And His throne shall be established in this place." (When our team was in Hongdae a couple of days later, Pastor Joanne also felt the Spirit's presence as we walked in this same area.) It confirmed to me again that Hongdae was the place he had sent us.

My time in Hongdae was unlike anything I had experienced before. As we walked down that center street, my heart was pounding, and I began weeping. It felt like my heart was being calibrated with His heart for Korea's younger generation. Is this what the making of a mother's heart feels like? I wondered. It is important to be led by the spirit, and Jinho provided inspired leadership at key moments. When he saw that I had become emotional, he found a second-story balcony where we could go. From that spot, I had a birds-eye view of the crowd where I could pray. It was just where I needed to be. Tears flowed as I prayed from my heart.

In the same way, the Spirit helps us in our weakness.
We do not know what we ought to pray for,
But the Spirit himself intercedes for us through wordless groans.
— Romans 8:26

October 12, 2016 — Mission base: Hongdae, sweet Hongdae

First it was just I. With Jinho, we were two. When the team arrived, we would be eight women and occasionally Jinho, who called our team "The Angels." He and I arrived first at the Airbnb in Hongdae. When we found the rental, there was some confusion about the passcode we needed to gain entry. After several phone calls, we finally got into the apartment. There were good reasons why the disciples were sent out two by two. Again, I was thankful for Jinho's help.

It was good to see my teammates when they arrived late from Malaysia. After months of team conference calls, we were finally together in Korea! Jinho helped carry luggage to the third floor before taking his long ride home on the subway. He serves others well.

Compared to my hotel in Seoul's busy city center, our third-story Airbnb is located in a quieter, neighborhood. We share three small bedrooms, two bathrooms, a modest living/dining area, and a simple, one-counter kitchen. Our team's humble abode is our place for rest, worship, prayer, and refueling. It is not my modern downtown hotel with its lavish breakfast buffet, but our simple apartment is intimate. Stores, taxis, and subways are just a block away. The team arrived tired and hungry and ordered Korean food at 1:00 a.m.

I am thankful to be an urban missionary with indoor plumbing and Internet service. Seoul is the most Internet-connected city in the world. Our home base is cozy and is located on the edge of the surrounding urban area, near Hongdae, where we will focus our ministry. Jinho has been a Godsend. He is helpful and adaptable and adjusts his schedule to support me. I appreciate the way he takes care of the details so that I am free to look, pray, listen, and process. I pinched myself several times again today as I realized, I am in Korea!

Reflection: Where do you need support in your life or ministry? Ask for it.

Good Morning from Hongdae

I hear the buzz of activity this morning: eggs being scrambled, women talking, and hair dryers humming. Today's planned activities are worship and prayer time, a visit to a missionary cemetery, grocery shopping, sightseeing, and a late-night prayer time on the Mapo Bridge.

We will join other locals who minister on the Mapo "Suicide Bridge," where many young people have ended their lives. They usually jump from the bridge at night, so that is when we plan to be there. There are rescue boats nearby to pull them out, but the victims sometimes drown before they can be saved. We are carriers of hope. We will pray for a release of abundant life and peace where too many have felt hopelessness and despair. We will pray that the assignment of death and suicide be cancelled and that hope and peace will be released in that place.

Reflection: What person, or group of people, need to be freed from hopelessness and despair? Where are you called to be a carrier of hope?

A Prayer for the Mapo Bridge

"May supernatural transformation come to the Mapo Bridge, so it will become a place of restoration, forgiveness, and healing. May the deep wounds inflicted by those who have committed suicide be replaced with healing for their family and friends, children, parents, and spouses. May His mercy fill the void that is left in the hearts of those who have grieved the loss of the people they loved. I ask that the waters of the Han River be cleansed and will no longer be waters of death but waters flowing with life. Amen."

I am processing many thoughts and emotions in this new-to-me country. I have appreciated having my own bedroom. The day began early for me. I used five tissues to wipe my tears. I prayed and cried, and wrote and cried. Tears were both healing and joyful. As I wept, I felt surrounded by His comforting love. My heart overflowed with gratefulness.

The next four days, we will be busy with a variety of ministry opportunities. I am now functioning as part of a team. It has been important to remain prayerful to maintain an esprit de corps. This has required loving teamwork and sensitivity to one another's needs. I see we are unified and supportive of each another. Together, we make a good team.

"The Angels" shared our first lunch in a basement restaurant in Hongdae. There are many underground spaces in this densely developed city. I ate some delicious samgyetang (삼계탕), an authentic

Korean chicken soup known for being healthful. At the restaurant, there was a San Francisco Giants baseball game on the television. The Giants were my team when I grew up in the San Francisco Bay Area in California. It is the little "kisses" like this that have cheered me while I am far from home.

Letter to Jinho

Good morning, Jinho.

I am enjoying this peaceful neighborhood setting in Hongdae while my teammates are still sleeping. I ended up with a private room, which is such a gift to me. My heart is overflowing with intense impressions and memorable images from yesterday. I have a desire to somehow capture my experiences on paper. Glimpses of beautiful moments from yesterday flow through my mind. My heart feels tender as I ask Him, "Are you sure you picked the right person for this assignment?" I have been teetering on the edge of feeling overwhelmed much of the past twenty-four hours.

Yesterday's amazing time made me feel like my heart could survive this journey to your country. Being surrounded by young sons and daughters in traditional Joseon apparel helped bring to life my mission as a "Mother of Asia" and made it feel more real. Praying for Song Jae In and her reaching out to take my hand with her tender, gifted hands was so special. I felt so happy that His love led us to her. Thank you for interpreting the Father's heart, as prayers flowed through me to her. I loved seeing her touched by His love.

I pray that your people will be set free from the things that hold them back so they can fully realize what they were created for and will reach their potential. Like the beauty of the mirrored reflections in the pond surrounding the Gyeonghoeru Palace, I want to be a beautiful reflection of my Creator. I want to be a catalyst for people to experience their own uniqueness and discover the future that is planned for them. I believe that, as each of us discovers our path, we will bring our Creator the greatest glory.

Thank you for accompanying me on this journey. This is obviously an intense adventure for my heart, and it is only day five. I don't want my vulnerability to bring defeat or cause any doubt in me. I trust the One who knows what He is doing, and I trust that my trip here has been being directed. He does all things well. I was sent, and I am surrounded by His love. As the worship song says: "He's a good, good father."

There are many impressions dancing in my mind and heart this morning. I feel like His child running through a meadow, trying to catch my beautiful butterflies. I am thanking Him for the gift of you, Jinho. Only God can truly know the depth of gratitude I feel. Because of His gift, I feel loved. I know you could compose a beautiful musical score to accompany the song of my heart. Thank you for loving others so well. You are special.

Linda

Jinho's response:

Thank you for your beautiful message, Linda. I hope you had enough rest at the new shelter. I was so surprised by yesterday's trip as well. God prepared the right people at the right positions and the right times. The painter said she's forty-one years old on the picture book, but she looked like she has pure eyes and heart and is blessed like you. And the water at the pond reminded me of the old saying of the Jews: "As above, as below." I hope we can contribute to the kingdom He lives in both in heaven and on the Earth.

Thank you and your team so much for all the wonderful prayer for my country and especially the young kids who are seeking God's love and the nonbelievers who need more of His warm care. I hope you continue on this great journey safely and full of joy through God's blessing. I'll see you soon when you have available time.

Jinho

October 12, 2016: Stroll around Yanghwajin Foreign Missionary Cemetery

After a full day and late night of ministry yesterday, my teammates are still snuggled in their beds. I woke up early this morning and have used almost a full iPhone battery writing and connecting with people in the USA. Having time for writing and processing has been a gift.

Yesterday we walked seven miles and climbed twenty-two flights of stairs. There is now a piece of duct tape (better than a regular bandage) covering a large blister on my foot. Tomorrow I will wear my sturdier Nike walking shoes. I will not be gaining weight on this trip; I will return home stronger than when I arrived.

How beautiful on the mountains are the feet of
those who bring good news, who proclaim peace,
who bring good tidings...
— Isaiah 52:7

Yesterday we scouted out the land and visited the Yanghwajin Foreign Missionary Cemetery (양화진 외국인 선교사 묘원). The death of Presbyterian minister John Heron in July 1890 is what prompted the small but growing foreign community in Seoul to look for a proper location for burials. Dr. Horace Allen acquired the land rights of the bluff overlooking the Han River. He called it Yanghwajin, named for an old ferry crossing that once existed nearby. The site for the cemetery already had historical significance because, in 1839, a number of French Catholic missionaries were put to death there. In 1866, a number of Korean Catholics were also killed in a mass execution on the nearby riverbank. It is a very important place for the history of Korean Christianity, where the footprints of missionaries were left long before my feet walked here.

Yanghwajin is known as the Foreign Missionary Cemetery because of the number of foreign missionaries buried there: 221 adults and 113 children. (These figures do not include the 23 known unmarked graves or the unknown number of Korean children from the Anglican orphanages who are buried on the upper slope of the Anglican plot.) Known nationalities include: Austria, Belgium, Canada, France, Germany, Italy, Japan, Korea, New Zealand, the Philippines, Russia, the United Kingdom, and the United States of America.

On the other side of Yanghwajin is the Protestant martyrs' shrine, because of the many Protestant missionaries buried there. The "100th Anniversary Memorial Church" was established in Yanhwajin to commemorate a century of missionary work in Korea.

I became emotional as I read the tombstones of those buried there. They felt called to come, and they literally laid down their lives for Korea and her people. Among the notable people buried there were:

Homer Hurlbert (1863-1949) — American missionary and journalist whose headstone says: *"I would rather be buried in Korea than in Westminster Abbey."*

Ernest Bethell (1872-1909) — Founder of Daehan Maeil Sinbo and who died after being imprisoned by the Japanese army or exposing abuses against Korean civilians.

George Henry Rue, MD. (1899-1993) — His tombstone reads: *"I did not come to Korea as a tourist. I came to this land to give my whole body and even my bones, to be buried in Korea. If a wolf attacks Koreans, I will not run away, as hired shepherds would do. Rather, I am a missionary who would give his life for the sheep. I have never treated my patients lightly. I have done my best to treat each patient, whether it was President Syngman Rhee or a poor farmer's wife."*

Horace Grant Underwood (1859-1916) — Founder of the Seoul YMCA, Saemunan Presbyterian Church, and what eventually became Yonsei University. His tombstone reads: *"Horace G. Underwood may be considered one of the earliest pioneers of Korean missions. He came to Korea on Easter Sunday in April of 1885 at the age of twenty-six. He actively engaged in mission work through mission trips, inviting junior missionaries to Korea, translating the Bible into Korean, and establishing Saemoonan Church, Kyungshin School, and Yonsei University. Through these activities and more, during his thirty-one years of service as a missionary in Korea, he greatly influenced many aspects of the Korean Church and society. It is difficult to find events of the early years of Korea mission in which he was not involved. Seven members of the Underwood family, spanning four generations, including H.G. Underwood and his wife, Lillian Horton, are buried at*

Yanghwajin. A memorial also stands here in honor of the Underwood family and John Thomas Underwood."

My heart was deeply moved as we quietly strolled the cemetery grounds. I read the tombstones and learned about the missionaries who began coming to Korea in 1837. In the far-right corner of the cemetery was a particularly touching scene — the tiny headstones of infants and children, some without a name and only "Infant" inscribed on their stone. I was not expecting to have such a profound experience at the missionary cemetery. I asked myself the question: What sacrifice might I be asked to make for Korea? The prayer on one monument said it well:

"Oh, I pray that I may be faithful and not mind about the success."
1890 September 14

Reflection: What sacrifice might you be asked to make for a city, a nation, or a people?

Staying Open to His Leading

Before we came to Korea, our team was advised to hold our agendas loosely. Our plans to go to the Mapo Bridge last night were postponed until Thursday night from 12:00 midnight to 2:00 a.m. Instead, the team will minister to the youth on the streets of Hongdae. We remain open to unexpected opportunities and divine appointments. It is good to be flexible.

Yesterday we ministered to people through prayer. Part of the

Top to Bottom: *Yanghwajin Painting by Jeong Seon (1676-1759)*

Ruby Kendrick Headstone: "If I had a thousand lives to live, Korea should have them all." Ruby Kendrick

team was out until after 3:00 a.m. last night. Before I came to Korea, I was directed, during prayer, to guard my health so I could go the distance. If I got tired, I could feel free to stay home. I remembered my doctor's advice when I was recovering from chronic fatigue years ago. "Linda, you have to pace yourself; you cannot sprint a marathon," he said. Last night I stayed home with Lynn, a lady in our group who had terrible swelling in her legs. We spent the evening sharing stories and encouraging one another.

Today's agenda is to "pray and play." We will worship, prayer-walk the four corners of Hongdae, and undoubtedly encounter some surprises. My cellphone battery is already down to twelve percent. I need to get dressed and cook breakfast this morning. It is 10:14 a.m., and I hear no activity in the house yet.

Prayer request for the team: While we are in the midst of this large population, please pray that our eyes will see specific individuals. Crowds will come and go. We do not seek the multitudes, but we are on the lookout for "the one" who needs a personal encounter. We ask that people who need encouragement will be highlighted for us.

Reflection: May you see "the one" in the crowd who needs the love you carry.

October 13, 2016: Sent here to love

The team prayed as we walked the streets of Hongdae today — the area of Seoul we are focused on. Lynn had a vision yesterday of a "thumbs up." When we were praying at the four corners of Hongdae, she noticed a sign across the street that read "Thumbs

Up Coffee Shop," featuring the thumbs-up logo she had seen. We happily hurried to the café for refreshments. While we enjoyed our coffee-stop time, I began to draw one of my child-friendly pictures featuring a little house, mountains, a rainbow, flowers, and trees — a simple scene I have drawn many times. I felt like I was supposed to quickly finish the picture before we left the café. I had only a little time to begin coloring it in.

As the team moved on, we walked only a short distance before I saw a young boy in a wheelchair being pushed by his Eomma (mother). I felt I had drawn my picture for him. We approached the mother and young boy and could see that he had a cast protecting his broken leg. After asking the mother's permission, I gave her son the picture I had drawn. It brought a smile to his face. My teammate, Toupou, gave his mother money to buy them some ice cream. We prayed for the boy's healing and spoke a blessing to his mother. Our simple, loving gifts brought smiles to their faces. We were sent here to love people. His love never fails.

Tonight we went to the Mapo Bridge with two men from the Ocean City Church. They have been ministering on the bridge for the past year and have prevented some college students from ending their lives. For the past year, I prayed for the Mapo suicide bridge and have cried about the troubled youth in the college area. We were out from 11:00 p.m. until 2:00 a.m. Several on the team had anticipated our bridge-ministry opportunity for many months. It was good to join with other English-speaking urban ministers who also felt called to Korea's youth.

"Oh, my God, what level of desperation would cause someone to jump from this bridge into the dark waters of the Han River?" my heart asked. Along the top of the railings on the Mapo Bridge, there were printed messages, a final plea to those who felt desperate in the hope that they might realize the value of their life. There were sample family pictures and scripted messages to start a conversation and send love. Unfortunately, the Bridge of Life Project of 2012, which sought to reverse the tragic trend of jumping, had the opposite effect, with suicides increasing more than sixfold since the campaign began.

Emergency telephones were nearby, ready to receive 119 calls (America's 911) from hopeless individuals. A bronze sculpture of a young person being consoled by a grandfatherly adult had been placed in the middle of the bridge. Many calls for "Help!" have come from the Mapo Bridge, usually late at night, when suicides are most common. Some have been pulled from the water by rescuers in boats that patrol the area. But too many precious people, many of them youth, have been lost, and their God-given destiny drowned with them. "God help us to bring freedom to those held by the chains of death!" I cried.

Praying for Korea's Government

We prayed over the seat of government and for Korea's leaders today as we toured the lovely Presidential "Blue House" grounds. I thought the Korean National Intelligence Service (NIS) was going to remove our team from the tour due to our excessive laughter. We were definitely carriers of joy today. The security guards kept their eyes on us. I heard some encouraging words about how God goes before me, He is my rear guard, and He is with me. Just like the mountains protecting Seoul, He is wonderfully surrounding me. It was a simple message, but, accompanied by His presence, it brought tears to my eyes. He is so close that I felt his breath on my face today.

I am thankful to be among the company of people who are praying for Korea. I have sensed His deep love for this nation. He has chosen Korea as one of His "sheep nations." Years ago, when I was wishing to be a mother, I never imagined there would be a time in my life when I would carry a nation and its people in my womb. Life is full of unexpected blessings.

The Spirit of the Sovereign Lord is on me, because the
Lord has anointed me to proclaim good news to the poor.
He has sent me to bind up the brokenhearted, to proclaim
freedom for the release from darkness for the prisoners, to proclaim
the year of the Lord's favor and the day of vengeance of our God,
to comfort all who mourn, and provide for those who grieve in Zion

—

to bestow on them a crown of beauty instead of ashes,
the oil of joy instead of mourning, and a garment of praise
instead of a spirit of despair. They will be called oaks

of righteousness, a planting of the Lord
for the display of his splendor.
— Isaiah 61:1-3

Gyeongbokgung Palace

Our team went to the Gyeongbokgung Palace today, one of the most beautiful and the largest of Korea's five Grand Palaces. It was the home of the kings of the Joseon Dynasty and the kings' households, as well as the government of Joseon. The stunning palace was burned to the ground during the Japanese invasion of 1592 to 1598, and, for the next almost three centuries (273 years) the palace grounds were left in ruins. I prayed for healing from the sorrow this nation still carries due to its history of invasion and war.

In 1867, the palace was finally rebuilt on a grander scale. The restoration has been ongoing since 1990, and, in 1996, the Japanese Government General Building (of 1911), constructed during the Japanese occupation of Korea, was removed. Both the Heungnyemun Gate (in 2001) and the Gwanghwamun Gate (from 2006 to 2010) were reconstructed in their original architectural style and location. Reconstruction was completed on the Inner Court and the Crown Prince's residence. It was estimated that, by the end of 2009, twenty-five percent of the structures that were standing before the Japanese occupation of Korea were restored or rebuilt, at a great cost to Korea. Restoring their significant structures in this area was important because they are a symbol of Korea's national sovereignty.

The name of the Joseon Dynasty's main royal palace is "*GyeongBokgung* (경복궁)." *Gyeong* (경) means "longevity," *Bok* (복)

means "luck," and *Gung* (궁) means "palace" — and so the palace was named wishing the longevity of the Joseon Dynasty. The Korean story about their country's tragic destruction, their deep sorrow, and the courageous rebuilding they have accomplished is truly an amazing one. They are a resilient, hard-working people who, like the Phoenix, have risen from their ashes.

Reflection: What has the enemy destroyed in your life that needs to be rebuilt?

The Team's Last Supper

Tomorrow will be our last day together as a team. I have seen how precious every moment is while ministering in another country. It is important to stay alert and be present in each moment in order not to miss opportunities. Our time has gone quickly. Pastor Joann went to visit her mother in the southern city of Busan. We prayed together before she left. Parting was bittersweet. I was in awe as I remembered it was just five months ago that I first met Pastor Joanne and Janet in Southern California — and this week, we have been in Korea together. I felt thankful as I reflected on how I was led to them.

Our team shared a final supper together at the large indoor Gwangjang market next to the Cheonggyecheon Stream. Everyone, except for me, ate Korean common octopus (낙지) that was still swimming in its tank seconds before its legs were chopped off and fried. Pieces of the poor little octopus were wiggling on the plate when it was served. When it comes to Korean food, I admit that I am probably the least daring among us, but that is OK with me. In other ways, I am thankful He made me quite adventurous!

October 14, 2016: Joy in the journey

Today was another incredible day. As we were out and about, we had opportunities to love people. Relationships were formed. We continually asked to be led to people who needed to encounter His love. We were among large crowds of people today. In a city like Seoul, it could be difficult to know where to minister. We simply loved one person at a time as they were highlighted for us.

Our team knows how to love well. I felt honored to serve with them. Today's focus was also the restoration of our team and loving one another. Seoul is the third stop for my team members who ministered in Vietnam and Malaysia before they arrived in Korea. Long days and late nights in this urban setting are physically and emotionally demanding, especially for the more introverted among us, but we have been strengthened daily.

Seoul is densely populated, and the streets are crowded. As we moved about the city this week, we used various modes of transportation: bus, subway, taxi, car, train, and shoe power. I have put many miles on my Oregon Nikes. My iPhone has provided a daily mileage and stair-climbing total. I will have walked more than two hundred miles by the end of this trip. As an urban missionary in Korea, sturdy shoes and comfortable, attractive clothing have been good choices.

Tonight we went to the Korean spa (*jimjilbang*, 찜질방). Our bodies were restored as we soaked in hot baths, sat in saunas, and lay on warm rocks. Some of us were treated to invigorating body scrubs and relaxing massages. The cleansing time helped remove weariness and stress. As we prepared to leave the spa, there was an explosion of laughter in the distant corner of the room. Yep, it was my joyful teammates.

A cheerful heart is good medicine...
— Proverbs 17:22

There is an abundance of good restaurants here to choose from. Koreans are "foodies." We were treated to a luxurious lunch buffet with many healthful options. Our private dining room was a place of continual joy as we shared moments of hysterical laughter. When was the last time you laughed uncontrollably? Hang out with people who bring you joy. It does a body good.

Reflection: Who are the people in your life who bring you joy? Get better connected to joy in your life.

October 14, 2016: Post by Tim

"Dear support group: I had to call Linda today to let her know that her mom passed away at 12:22 p.m. this afternoon (10/14 here, 4:22 a.m. 10/15 in Korea). She could certainly use your prayers during this tender time. — Tim"

October 15, 2016: A day I will not forget

Tim called early today with sad news. "Your mommy passed away early this morning at 4:22 a.m. Korea time," he said. I was prepared for the possibility that I might not see my mom again, but I was also surprised to hear that she was gone. Her hip surgery had been successful, and I was encouraged to learn that mom was doing well. News of her death broke my heart.

When I shared the news of mom's passing with my teammates,

their common response was: "What?" I think we all assumed that, when we went where we were led, our loved ones at home would be protected. I was far from Oregon and felt conflicted because I could not be with my mother.

Precious in the sight of the Lord is the death of his faithful servants.
— Psalm 116:15

Thankfully, mom and I had already gone to the funeral home and made all her final arrangements together. Her last, generous request was that her body be donated to a medical school for research purposes. Right to the end, mom gave her all. After prayerful consideration, I decided she would want me to stay in Korea and not fly home. I will process my mother's passing here with my teammates.

Even as a writer, it is difficult to express my emotions. I loved my mom and treasured the final seven years we were able to spend together. I feel some comfort knowing she is now free from Alzheimer's disease. She is truly "at home," where her mind is clear

and her heart is at rest. Goodbye, precious Mom, until we meet again. *Reflection:* Do your loved ones know your wishes at your time of passing? Consider writing down your desires, and giving them a copy.

October 16, 2016: Gangnam style

After our team left, Janet and I met her mom, Sara, in Gangnam. We went grocery shopping at Shinsegae department store in a luxurious market in one of Seoul's most upscale areas. The store displays were lovely — Gangnam style at its best. The presentation of merchandise was exquisite. There were pretty fresh orchids for sale in the produce department, a variety of fresh fish swimming in huge tanks, and lovely bamboo brushes displayed in the personal-product area.

I was impressed with the warm, excellent service of Koreans in the first-class Gangnam store, with all the accoutrements of abundant wealth. In each department, female employees were dressed in pressed uniforms, waiting to serve customers. Sara chose the items she wanted, and the servers placed them in bags for her. At the checkout station, there were two lovely women wearing crisp white blouses and tailored suits. One woman handled the cash, and the other woman, wearing white gloves, bagged our groceries. A handsome Korean gentleman in a dark-blue suit, white shirt, and tie stood nearby ready to assist. I definitely felt like an urban missionary today.

What the Korean people have accomplished in the seventy years following the Korean War (1950-1953) is impressive. Through sacrifice and hard work, they rebuilt their country and established themselves as eleventh in the world's economies and the leading nation in technology. It is not obvious that Koreans are also struggling, but when I looked carefully, I could see their stress. They are hard workers who appear more industrious than relaxed. Since I was a young girl, I have been a people watcher who has studied emotions on faces. My mother would often catch me "watching" and say, "It's not polite to stare." There are many new faces to study in this populated city.

Thank you for your prayers

Though waves of emotions come in private moments, I am mostly at peace with my mom's passing. I am thankful she is no longer suffering from the confusion and sadness she experienced in her final months. This past year, it was especially hard to see her struggling to find words. One day, however, she clearly said, "I want to DO something!" Mom had a talent for serving and helping others. Then she leaned into me and said, "Let's get outta here." And so, she has.

In her last year, Alzheimer's disease gradually robbed mom of her memory, her abilities, and her quality of life. She slipped away from us a little bit at a time. I am thankful we made good memories and that our relationship ended well. I have no regrets — only overwhelming, flowing-with-warm-tears gratitude.

I am leaving busy Seoul to go stay with Janet and her parents in the mountains of Seojong, a cute country town on the Han River. Later Janet and I will return to my city-center hotel across the street from my favorite Namdaemun traditional marketplace. I have had some friendly encounters with a few shop owners, mostly with simple "Hellos" and smiles. Janet and I will prayer-walk several areas of the city, as we stay alert for divine appointments. Life here has been an adventure.

The Lord is my strength and my shield;
my heart trusts in him and he helps me.
My heart leaps for joy,
And with my song I praise him.
— Psalm 28:7

Reflection: Is there unfinished business in your life? Are there communications you need to deliver? This might be a good time to tie up any loose ends.

October 17, 2016: Asking for the nations

This is week two of my journey. Janet and I will be without our team this coming week. We will miss them all, but Jinho will occasionally join us. I have continued to pray for the seven mountains (arenas) of Korean culture: religion, education, family, government, media, arts and entertainment, and business, remembering that, in order for countries to experience a spiritual awakening, these areas need to experience change.

Reflection: Is there a nation(s) you feel called to? He says:

Ask of me, and I will make the nations as your inheritance,
the ends of the earth your possession.
— Psalm 2:8

October 18, 2016: Prayer-walking Seoul

After two and a half days of peaceful rest at the Juns' lovely mountain home, truly a place of refuge, Janet and I will return to Seoul today. We will prayer-walk Gangnam, Apgujeong-dong, Cheongdam-dong, and the entertainment district with its clubs, high-fashion stores, and entertainment companies.

It is hard to grasp or even speak about the heartbreaking reality that South Korea is the suicide capital of the world. These industrious, attractive people look so good on the outside. One needs to observe them with eyes of compassion to see the stress they carry on the inside. Though forty percent of Koreans profess to be Christians, others do not know they are His beloved sons and daughters. Discovering how deeply they are loved could bring freedom from their performance orientation and perfectionism. Competition, alcoholism, inadequacy, loneliness, greed, envy, selfish ambition, bullying and being bullied, class discrimination, hopelessness, addiction, and suicide — these are just some of the enemies they battle. I have been reminded of the following verse:

> *The Lord does not look at the things people look at. People look at*
> *the outward appearance but the Lord looks at the heart.*
> *— 1 Samuel 16:7*

As I people-watch here, I ask that I will be able to see their hearts. The Korean people are generally more reserved and private than are most Americans in the United States. I am asking for opportunities to get to know them heart to heart.

Lovely Seojong

Janet and her parents, Sara and Eddie, have been so welcoming. At their home, I have a private bedroom and bathroom with a heated bed and floors. They have blessed me with delicious, healthy meals and their love. Out my bedroom window, I have a view of the pretty mountains as I pray. I enjoy the fragrance and beauty of Sara's pink roses in the garden as we come and go. As I have gone with God, He has put me in pleasant places. I will remember this place and the Juns' kindness forever.

Janet and I spent time together in the garden of a coffee shop in town. The shop's eclectic décor included fresh flower bouquets on the tables, Thomas Edison light bulbs, chalk boards for drawing, antique oak furniture, polymer telephones, and groovy old radios. We both liked the vintage style that is also popular with Koreans. We will return to the Namdaemun Marriott hotel at city center, a good location for visiting Hongdae again. We continue to seek God's heart for the younger generation there. May we be guided and see clearly today. I am experiencing great peace, and I'm incredibly thankful for this opportunity. Sometimes I felt like I was walking and living in a surreal dream.

Reflection: When did you last smile at and greet a complete stranger? A love encounter can brighten the day of a dark, desperate soul.

October 19, 2016: The blessing of technology

To my precious friends and family, thank you for covering me in prayer. I have loved sharing this journey with you. I am thankful to be an urban missionary equipped with high-tech tools (an iPhone and iPad) for communicating with you from across the miles. Though the Internet speed is less dependable in the towns beyond the city center, Seoul is definitely Internet-connected. I needed better storage capacity on my iPhone and had to delete things to continue taking photos and videos. Jinho helped me get a temporary Korean phone number and a new SIM card for my iPhone. I have needed and appreciated his tech support.

In our remaining days, Janet and I will focus on Hongdae and the university district we are praying for. We will meet with a few pastors to share our vision for Hongdae. We are reaching out to the next generation with the hope of the good news. May these precious young Koreans discover and fulfill their destiny.

A Spiritual Awakening

We have seen a spiritual awakening coming to Korea and believe that many young missionaries will be sent from here to other countries in Asia and around the world. Tonight, we will meet with the talented American singer and missionary Joseph Butso. I am thankful for the night Jinho's and my path intersected with Joseph's when he was singing on a street corner in Itaewon. I look forward to seeing him again and learning how we can pray for his ministry in Korea.

Tomorrow, I head back to Oregon, USA. Our peaceful country home will provide the perfect setting for processing all I have seen and experienced. Our schedule has been full. A big blessing of this journey was meeting Jinho. He will be traveling back to Oregon with me to visit my beautiful state and soak up its peace.

Remember when I said that I would probably want to bring one of the cute Korean kids home with me? Well, I never imagined connecting with a six-foot two-inch tall creative — one of Korea's special sons. I love surprises!

Take delight in the Lord and he will
give you the desires of your heart.
— Psalm 37:4

Reflection: Who needs your love today — a text, an email, a card, or a call? If a name comes to your mind, I encourage you to follow through. Small acts of love can make a big difference in someone else's life.

October 19, 2016: My Korean adventure

I have wondered how my Korean adventure looks from afar. I asked my prayerful friends, "In just a few words, tell me how my trip looks from where you are." They responded with these fun words. I think they are sharing my experience!

Insightful
Enlightening
Culturally fascinating

Divinely orchestrated by God
Spiritual
Humbling
Healthy
Exciting
Appreciative
Artistic
Joyful in the journaling
Amazingly blessed and filled with riches

The kind of Holy Spirit journey we could all have for a lifetime!

October 20, 2016: Korea, you are beautiful

Good morning. This is my last full day in Korea. My heart feels thankful and melancholy as I prepare to leave. Janet and I said our "Goodbyes" and shared hugs last night. Our Korean journey together has been wonderful!

Yesterday was fun! Janet and I connected with various pastors, entertainers, and ministry leaders. It was good to meet others who have a similar heart and passion for Korea, especially for those in the younger generation. While pioneering in a new country, forming the right relationships has been important. It has been good to join in what others are already doing. There is strength in numbers and no need to "reinvent the wheel."

This morning I will meet Chris, an employee and board member for Jang Kuen Suk (JKS), the successful young Korean actor and the owner of Tree J Company. He was the lead actor in the K-Drama

You Are Beautiful who first drew me into the Korean arts-and-entertainment arena. Because of the influence these young Korean entertainers have, I have continued to pray that Keun Suk would be used to positively influence his culture. I look forward to having lunch with Chris and telling her about how Jang Keun Suk helped draw me to Korea. I was told that she speaks fluent English, which should make for good communication. I am anticipating more serendipitous events today. I feel strengthened by your prayers. Thank you, friends.

Reflection: Whom can you support or join with in the goal of blessing others? There is strength in unity and teamwork.

October 21, 2016: A divine appointment

2:03 a.m.: It looks like I will have to wait until I get home to fully enjoy sleeping again. My adrenaline has definitely been on overdrive. Today was another great day. I had the privilege of meeting Chris from Tree J Company, who works for Jang Keun Suk, one of the Korean entertainers I have prayed for this past year. She rode public transportation for two hours to meet me at my hotel and brought me a big bag of gifts. We took a taxi to a nice restaurant in Cheongdam-dong where the entertainers like to eat.

We shared a delicious meal in a trendy restaurant that is one of JKS's favorites. I told Chris my story about finding the Asian coin and hearing the words, "I am putting Asia on your path." I explained how my Korean adventure accelerated after I saw Keun Suk's K-Drama You Are Beautiful. Chris said that she had heard many fan stories and that mine was the best JKS story she had ever heard. She said she would definitely tell Jang Keun Suk how he captured my attention and drew me to Korea.

Chris and I shared our life stories and dreams. She grew up as a PK (preacher's kid), and we share the Christian faith. Her goals included writing projects and mentoring youth. Chris felt that our meeting was perfectly timed for her. I was happy I could encourage her. She is a talented, joyful, and kind person. I believe she will realize her dreams. While I was with Chris, I also felt like I was in the right place at the right time — another divine appointment.

"Sully," Prepared for His Mission

Later we met Jinho in Gangnam, where he and I went to see the American movie Sully, in an upscale theatre. I appreciated being able to watch an English-language film. It was an inspiring movie about Captain Chesley "Sully" Sullenberger III, who, on January 15, 2009, was forced to make an emergency landing on the Hudson River off Manhattan in New York City after a Canadian geese "bird strike" hit the engine of his US Airways Airbus A320. Sully successfully landed the plane in the river and saved all 155 passengers!

What impressed me the most about Captain Sully's successfully landing the plane in the Hudson was that his entire aviation career had prepared him for that moment. He was not only a seasoned pilot of almost four decades, but he had also helped to develop new protocols in airline safety. The movie's song lyrics in "Sully's Theme" said it well: "You were born for the storm you have to weather." Each of us has been uniquely prepared for our futures. As we receive today's training and capture the opportunities we have to learn and mature, we will be ready to meet the storms and challenges of our tomorrows. Seize the day.

> *...being confident of this, that he who began*
> *a good work in you will carry it on to completion...*
> — *Philippians 1:6*

Championing Others

In the past few weeks, I have had opportunities to encourage others, particularly those in Korea's arts-and-entertainment industry. Before I came here, I was told that I was "A Mother of Asia." I pondered what her role was. I am realizing that a mother is a wise friend who supports the calling of others, especially those in the younger generation. She is a helper, a prayer partner, and a loving champion. Mothers can sometimes see who one is created to be. Then she supports them as they prepare to launch into their future. When I return to Oregon, I will continue to pray for Korea and the destiny of her rising generation.

One day when I was talking to Tim, I told him I was wondering how I could encourage Jinho. Tim said this in response to my contemplations: "You are in the perfect position to champion Jinho." And that was the defining word I needed to hear — "champion." I will look for ways to champion and encourage Jinho.

My bags are packed, and I am ready to go. I am sad about leaving, but I look forward to hosting Jinho on his first trip to Oregon. Goodnight, prayer warriors.

Reflection: Who in your life are you perfectly positioned to champion?

October 22, 2016: My "WOW! Journey" continues

Surprise, I just got bonus days in Korea! This morning Jinho discovered that his passport had expired last month, so we rescheduled our departure. I received the gift of another week in Korea. I wonder what surprises await me?

I checked out of my hotel yesterday and am, once again, soaking up the peace and quiet of the Juns' lovely mountain setting. My "Wow! Journey" continues, and sleeping is still challenging. My Korean adventure has been stimulating for all of my senses. I have been operating on part joy, part inspiration, and part raw adrenaline — it's not a bad combination, but definitely not a sustainable one for a long-distance race.

Yesterday I visited a district of Seoul called Dongdemun, with its unique, young-at-heart fashion styles and K-Pop talent. Seoul is one of Asia's hottest fashion cities. I have enjoyed seeing the store displays, architecture, and clothing styles, which are different from the relaxed apparel of "hoodies," blue jeans, and the popular casual wear of America's Pacific Northwest. At home, we dress more for warmth and comfort, and most Oregon women prefer their Nikes on country roads to high heels on city sidewalks.

I am learning so much about the culture when I am out and about with the Korean people. It has been a blessing to have Jinho guide me through the various districts in the city. I have made some amazing connections during my last few days of this breathtaking adventure.

Reflection: Where is it difficult for you to wait for something to happen in your life? His timing is often different, and usually better, than our timing. What you perceive as your setback may just be a divine setup.

October 23, 2016: Ahhhhh

Resting in lovely Seojong again. Ahhhhh…perfect. I have a new mom. Eomma Sara washed my clothes and made me a healthy salmon lunch today. I felt loved.

Reflection: Is there someone in your life who needs the love of a spiritual mother or father? Your love can fill a void and make a difference.

October 24, 2016: Making connections

Today Janet and I will leave our family sanctuary and head back to Seoul. Jinho will meet us at the Seoul Station for our two-and-a-half-hour ride on the KTX high-speed train to the southern coastal city of Busan, the second-largest city in Korea, with three million people. We will meet Pastor Joanne from our team, who is there visiting her parents. I anticipate a time of celebration as we share stories about our Korean adventure.

I am thankful to have had restful days interspersed with "WOW!" days. I feel ready to experience my final days here. When we return to Seoul tonight, Janet and I will meet Chris from the Ocean City Church in Hongdae at 11:00 p.m. for street ministry. We plan to visit the outdoor plazas, where the young people hang out with friends and play music.

After our ministry time, Janet and I will spend the night at the *jimjilbang* (찜질방). a bathhouse with gender-segregated hot baths and saunas, a co-ed floor, a cool room, hot rooms, a lounging area with a big-screen TV, and a café. They permit overnight sleeping, Asian-style, on floor mats. America needs the same rejuvenating spas.

Tomorrow Janet and I will have lunch with Jinho and his Korean mother, Younghee, at a restaurant in the Buddhist district. We will share healthful food in a private room. Such a formal introduction is important in the Korean culture.

> *Ask and it will be given to you;*
> *seek and you will find;*
> *knock and the door will be opened to you.*
> *— Matthew 7:7*

Sarah and Eddie, Janet's parents, prayed for Janet and me today. Eddie prayed in Korean. I recorded his precious prayers for Jinho to translate later. They are people of great faith. Their home has been like heaven on Earth. They have provided generously and lovingly cared for me. They expressed their appreciation for my prayers for Korea and my support for Janet as she begins to launch into her full-time ministry.

Reflection: Koreans are a praying people, which is one of the reasons they had such an impressive rebuilding of their country after the devastating Korean War of the 1950s. Prayer is a key to restoration in your life. Continue to ask, seek, and knock. You may not receive a 100-fold return on your prayers, but do keep praying.

October 25, 2016: Another adventurous day

Today we rode the KTX high-speed train to Busan on the southern coast of Korea — the city known as "The Little San Francisco of Asia." Busan reminded me of San Francisco, California, my beloved "City by the Bay," close to Redwood City, where I grew up. The Gwang-an suspension bridge (or Diamond Bridge) that connects Haeundae-gu to Suyeon-gu is 4.6 miles long, the second-longest bridge in Korea and is similar in style to San Francisco's Golden Gate Bridge. Busan also has small hills that rise from its bay, lined with cargo ships and fine-sand beaches. My heart was warmed by the similarities between San Francisco and the lovely coastal city of Busan. I hope to visit there again someday.

The KTX high-speed train provided a quiet, scenic, and comfortable ride. I enjoyed my views of the Korean countryside and used train time to catch up on communications and relax. We met Pastor Joanne and went to one of Busan's popular, traditional outdoor markets, which offered many appealing options for lunch. I chose one of my favorite Korean dishes, a gluten-free mung bean pancake with veggies inside called *bindae-tteok* (빈대떡).

After lunch, we walked along the beach, which was empty on the overcast October day. I imagined how lively the pretty Busan beaches must be on a warm, sunny day. We had a sweet time of prayer there. At a coffee shop with an open-air second floor facing the Diamond Bridge, we enjoyed the lovely view as we shared stories. It was inspiring to debrief with Pastor Joanne about the experiences we all had.

We rejoiced in the divine appointments, the unexpected blessings, and even my migraine headache, which led Jinho and me to Itaewon, which was where we'd met the American singer Joseph Butso. Pastor Joanne said, "Praise God for your migraine headache!" Well, we are encouraged to rejoice in all things. Joanne, Janet, and others had prayed about their Korea mission for quite a while. It was good to pause, reflect, and give thanks for all we had experienced.

Reflection: Take time to give thanks for the blessings in your life.

Street Ministry

We shared our "Goodbyes" and group hug before riding the train back to Seoul. Jinho went on his way, and Janet and I headed for street ministry with Chris in Hongdae. We spent most of our ministry time, from 11:00 p.m. to 1:00 a.m. hanging out with the young people in an outdoor plaza, listening to them play guitars and sing. When a non-Korean foreign man persistently hustled me, I wished Jinho were there to handle him, but Janet proved to be a watchful ministry partner.

After our time with the young people, Janet and I went to the Siloam Spa, where we soaked in hot baths and slept in a darkened room on beds made of warm, smooth stones. We enjoyed some restoration time after our long-but-good day. Jinho later said that Chris, Janet, and I had gone on our "You've-Lost-Your-Mind Ministry," since we were out in the middle of the night with the Korean kids. I had to admit that it was an unusual time of day for ministry, but we needed to be out when and where the young people were. It was a long, rich day of traveling and connecting.

Reflection: What young person needs you to just listen without giving them any advice?

October 26, 2016: He orchestrates our lives

We will rest this morning before our final day of connecting here. Janet, Jinho, and I are invited for lunch at "The Jokbal," Yoon's family restaurant in Dangsan, near Hongdae. Yoon is a young man we met the day that "The Angels" and Jinho prayer-walked the four corners of Hongdae.

Yoon, a young man with a bright smile, was in a time of transition. He had just unplugged from his Internet life to pursue his musical interests and to help manage his parents' restaurant near Hongdae. He said he wanted to create "beats" for hip-hop music and that he was setting up a small studio for himself. He caught Janet's attention when she saw him sitting on some steps wearing an "Oregon" sweatshirt in the yellow-and-green school colors of the University of Oregon, where he was a student for a year. The U of O in Eugene, Oregon, is just an hour south of where I live.

Yoon said it was unusual for him to be in that area of Hongdae. He just felt like sitting in that spot. Soon after he sat down, our team came along. Three of us were able to encourage Yoon: a male musician, a woman from Oregon, and a young woman from Korea who could follow up with him — just the right, handpicked team. After lunch, we prayed for Yoon. I felt led to share the scripture from Jeremiah 29:11: "I know the plans I have for you...plans to give you a hope and a future." Yoon was encouraged and said that was his favorite Bible verse.

Reflection: Consider going on a treasure hunt today. Boldly ask to meet someone who needs your love, and be on the lookout for him or her.

No fear.   *People care.*
Don't worry my friend. *Things will be all right!*
God knows your name and address, and He sees where you are.
He is orchestrating the details of your life on your behalf.
He can send his people right to where you are,
to encourage you and love on you.
Oh, He really does care
about you!

Today we were back in Hongdae, on a mission to bring hope and life and to pray that the destiny of the next generation would be fulfilled. I wrote this prayer in my journal:

My Morning Prayer:

"Let me carry your deep love to the Korean people, a love that will cause them to embrace who they were created to be. Let me speak words of life to each person's identity and not words that merely flatter or feed egos that are hungry for the approval of men. Set them free to pursue their passions and the desires of their hearts and to discover their true destiny. Amen."

Prepare for Your Future

Janet and I will meet with a group of mature missionaries today. Dr. Abraham Lee and his two sons started a ministry called "Care Corner," in a building in Hongdae with a café at street level and the Care Corner ministry auditorium underground. A couple hundred young people meet there for worship, a scripted movie presentation with a professional-grade production, a discussion time with the actors and actresses, and a rich teaching by Dr. Lee. Jinho joined us that night at Care Corner, and we were all impressed with the excellent outreach.

For many years, Dr. Lee had a dentistry business. While he worked as a dentist, he pursued his passion to mentor young people in the Hongdae area. For twelve years, he had prayerfully prepared himself. During our dinner meeting, he emphasized the importance of spending time in prayer. I certainly agreed with him, since much prayer had also brought me to that moment in time.

...I urge you to live a life worthy of the calling you have received.
— Ephesians 4:1

When Janet and I had dinner with Dr. Lee and a few other pastors, Pastor Eddie, Janet's father, told them my mother had died a few days earlier. I do not speak much Korean, but I recognized the moment when Eddie told the pastors the heartbreaking news of my "Eomma's" passing. When they all looked at me, I saw compassion in their eyes. I had wondered if that would be the moment when the Koreans would think I was a dishonoring daughter who had abandoned my mother in her time of need. I was relieved to see that they did not judge me. Instead, because I left my mom at an emotional time, they believed I was a sent one who was serious about my calling to Korea. The pastors thanked me for my willingness to leave my country to come pray for Korea and their young people.

After dinner, we went with Eddie and several of the pastors to a meeting at a house of prayer they were establishing. In the more male-dominant Korean culture, Janet and I respectfully supported them in silent prayer as the men prayed about their decision. That night, they decided to sign a lease agreement for the space where they had been meeting and praying.

"In every situation, ask yourself: to whom am I submitting."
Watchman Nee

I could see that the pastors had pure hearts and that their love for one another had unified them. As they sought wisdom and direction, they built their Hongdae outreach on a solid foundation through prayer. I felt privileged to meet them. Dr. Lee was a gracious man who spoke enough English to communicate with me, though, at one point, he humbly and humorously said, "Speaking so much English is hurting my brain." I loved praying for people who were pioneering a new ministry.

Reflection: Take a minute to pray that you will be prepared, and led, to both the known and the unknown opportunities in your future.

October 27, 2016: Precious final days

We are in our final countdown before leaving for the USA. I look forward to sharing my beautiful Oregon with Jinho. As the bumper sticker says, "I ADOREGON!" Your prayers have carried me, and I have loved writing to you each day. I look forward to reading these posts and reflecting on my trip in the months and years to come. This trip to Korea has been a high point in my life and a new beginning for me — and, I believe — for Jinho, too.

There will be many things to reflect on and pray about when I leave Korea. On this first "WOW! Journey," God has orchestrated what no man or woman could have. He answered prayers and blessed in the physical what He showed me during prayer. We walked many miles as we prayed up and down the streets, across bridges, and in various districts and neighborhoods as we scouted out the land. Everywhere we walked, we left the imprint of our prayers. As we prayed, we believed we received what we asked for. I met many special people and experienced the local culture. We brought hope where despair had clouded vision and robbed many young people of their lives.

Something deep was birthed in me. I have felt God's heart for Korea and her people. He has kept me close. Our team prayed for true and lasting peace for the entire Korean peninsula. I am hopeful that someday there will be a reunification of North and South Korea. We prayed for her protection. We truly believe that "It's Korea's time" for a spiritual awakening.

His Burden Is Light

Though there is much about the culture and people that looks perfect on the outside, I have become acquainted with the Korean people's environmental and internal stressors. It is an extremely competitive, futuristic society that does not accept much imperfection in its people. Intense expectations are placed on the younger generation to perform. They are driven from an early age to be at the top-of-the-game, but there are only so many places at the top. So, life in Korea, particularly Seoul, can be exhausting, and at the same time fascinating.

Education is in the highest position with the Korean people. Beginning at a young age, in addition to their regular schooling, their youth attend a variety of private institutes for specialized learning that often costs thousands of dollars each month. Students are disciplined by teachers and guided by parents who expect them to be among the best. The younger Korean generation lives under great pressure. They are pushed by a competitive culture that does not permit much freedom to choose their own life path, much less pursue what they feel passionate about.

The American values of "life, liberty, and the pursuit of happiness" are important elements of our Declaration of Independence and are freedoms the people of the United States value. The Korean way is predominantly "study, study, study, work hard, sacrifice, and be successful." Success is mostly measured by educational achievement, economic standing, and a flawless, youthful appearance. Their life is not easy. It is undeniable that Koreans have paid a high price to live under intense cultural pressures. Many times, I saw high school students and businessmen riding the subways home as late as midnight.

> *Come to me, all you who are weary and burdened,*
> *and I will give you rest. Take my yoke upon you*
> *and learn from me for I am gentle and humble in heart,*
> *and you will find rest for your souls,*
> *for my yoke is easy and my burden is light.*
> *— Matthew 11:28-30*

In this land of great expectations, Korea is number one in workaholics, work-related alcohol consumption, and plastic surgery. Americans are also guilty of working too hard, and there are far too many people in the USA who expect government assistance and feel entitled to their freedoms. While I had great respect for what Koreans have accomplished through their teamwork and rebuilding, my heart was saddened to see the intense environment they have lived in, the backlash of the many demands that are placed on them.

My trip to Korea taught me more about abiding in Him. In my quiet, solitary moments, He was there, listening, comforting, and guiding me. Without His peaceful presence, I could not have thrived here. I was grateful to be reminded that I am unconditionally loved and accepted for whom I am, and not for what I do. He delights in me. Because He was with me, I was able to love people and see my calling being fulfilled. My journey to Korea stretched me and taught me the importance of going where He led me, for purposes that He revealed day by day. I wanted what He wanted. As Pastor Frank at Hope Church in Albany, Oregon, said, "You cannot have destiny without devotion." Without a doubt, my heart and my life are His.

If I had continued to focus on the children I did not have, or on my unfulfilled desire to be a mother, I could have gone through life disappointed, bitter, and missing many opportunities. He enabled me to stay open to His plans and purposes. A big turning point came when I chose to surrender my desires and trust in His plans. Trusting was a continual decision and ushered me into an amazing, ever-changing life that was beyond what I ever expected or hoped for. It was good to dream, but it was more important to stay open to the possibility that my life would play out much differently than I had envisioned or wanted it to.

> *Many are the plans in a person's heart.*
> *But it is the Lord's purpose that prevails.*
> *— Proverbs 19:21*

Reflection: What dream or desire do you need to hold loosely?

♪

Video: *"Joseph Butso singing gospel songs in downtown Korea,"*
and Joseph Butso, "I Can See Your Voice 3"

Song: *"Good Good Father," by Chris Tomlin*

Song: *"Amazing Grace (My Chains Are Gone)," by Chris Tomlin*

Song: *"Well Done," by The Afters*

Song: *"Reckless Love," by Cory Asbury*

Song: *"Memory of the Wind," by Naul (바람추억)*

Video on Vimeo.com: *"Seoul Wave," by Brandon Li*

Video: *Seungyeol Lee main theme song from K-Drama Incomplete Life*

41.
HEADING FOR OREGON

On our way to the airport, I reflected on my time in Korea. Tears rolled down my cheeks again. I was in awe and felt deep gratitude for the opportunity I had been given to partner in His plans and purposes for Korea. I received a vision of Hongdae. I was connected to my team. He sent me confirming signs that it was all His doing. Our days were wonderfully directed. Our needs were bountifully provided for. Where He guided, He provided. My Mother Heart was stirred. I was leaving Korea a more-experienced urban missionary with Jinho, who had shared my rich maiden voyage with me. We referred to our Korea time as our "Wow! Adventure." Later we would discover that blessings were waiting to be poured out on Jinho, too.

"Shared joy is a double joy; shared sorrow is half sorrow."
Swedish Proverb

To all of you reading this book, I believe there are unimagined, meaningful opportunities ahead for you, too. To my Baby Boomer and senior readers, I encourage you to remain hopefully expectant. It could just be that some of your best days are still to come. I was sent to a country I had never planned to go to. I have an active imagination and have dreamed some big dreams, but my Korea adventure was "exceedingly and abundantly beyond all I could ask or imagine" (Ephesians 3:20). God loves the world. He may just send you to the people of other lands to tell them about His great love.

I was sent on an unexpected journey. My heart was stretched this way and that, enlarging my capacity to love others. As I toured the South Korean cities of Seoul, Busan, and Seojong, I experienced His presence and felt His love. He touched my heart and made my days purposeful. Many times, tears came unexpectedly. I cannot remember a time when I cried as much as I did during my three weeks in Korea. My heart was touched when I saw the young people and witnessed the stress and loneliness on their faces. Many times, I felt a profound compassion for people whose names I did not know. A deep love was birthed in my heart for Korea and her people.

Going to a foreign country opened me wider to His overwhelmingly great love. I had moments of discovery and received blessings and surprises every day. My time in Korea was planned and lovingly choreographed, right down to the smallest detail. It was inspiring to experience how much He truly loves us all. There were times when my heart felt completely and wonderfully apprehended. I left Korea a different person. I assure you, right here and now, that you cannot imagine where He might send you or what He wants to do through you. We are all conduits of an amazing, unlimited love. Like a mighty river, His love can flow from us to bless others.

Taste and see that the Lord is good;
blessed is the one who takes refuge in him.
— Psalm 34:8

Before we left for Oregon, Jinho's Korean mother, Younghee, invited me to lunch. It was an important meeting. On the way to the restaurant, I stopped at the flower shop and bought her a bouquet of bright pink roses, her favorite color. The healthy lunch was beautifully prepared, and our time together was peaceful. Jinho and Janet interpreted the conversation for me, and we ended our meal with a sweet time of prayer. My heart connected with Younghee's heart that day.

After lunch, Jinho, Younghee, and I walked around Insadong and looked in some shops. Younghee showed her appreciation for my kindness to Jinho by buying me some gifts. In a shop with many lovely scarves, she insisted on buying me several. I appreciated her generous spirit and her trust in me. Before we separated, she prayed a special blessing over me in Korean. I later learned that, when Jinho was young, his mother had a dream that one day he would live in a foreign country. I feel honored to have met Jinho, a man who was birthed by his Korean mother. I appreciated her gifts and her prayers for me. Like a true mom, her final request was, "Please find him a job."

As she walked off, I wondered how she must have felt. I sensed her love for her son and her courage as she entrusted him to a woman she had just met. My observation of natural mothers and champions is that they fight for those they love. Moms love their children and then release them to fulfill their destiny. In honor of Jinho's mother, Younghee, I will do my best to love him and to champion his true destiny, however I am led.

42.
OUR ADVENTURE
CONTINUES

We left bustling Seoul, South Korea, and arrived in peaceful Oregon. It was good to recover lost sleep and ponder my time in Korea. Jinho took hundreds of photographs as we rode along the coastline, hiked in forests by cascading waterfalls, gazed into blue pools, walked along the Metolius River during a full moon, and admired beautiful sunsets and rainbows from our porch. At pristine Clear Lake in the Cascade Range, where ducks skimmed the still water, we felt inspired. Jinho said he always wanted to be a countryman; our home is located on "Countryman Circle." Oregon's nature was a healing balm that brought restoration to us all.

During his visit, I learned that Jinho had wanted to pursue a Master's degree in composition and film scoring. We visited the music department at nearby Oregon State University (OSU) to see what music degrees they offered. They did not have a Master's program in composition, but we were told that Western Oregon University (WOU) had an MM degree in composition and film scoring. The next day, we went to the WOU campus, where Professor Dirk gave us a tour of the music department. He welcomed Jinho applying to their graduate program.

After considering his options, Jinho decided to apply for the

WOU Master's program to pursue his interest in media composition. When he sent his application, which included samples of his original compositions, he was accepted. He received a full scholarship for his first term and a graduate assistantship (GA) for the remaining terms, which covered tuition and helped Jinho build his composer's toolbox. Where the doors opened, there was provision. The adventure continued.

The day after Thanksgiving, Jinho left for Korea and planned to return to Oregon in the spring to begin the WOU Master's composition/film scoring program. As Shakespeare said, "Parting is such sweet sorrow." As we anticipated his return, I prepared Jinho's bedroom and bathroom. I painted tan over the blue walls and bought a masculine desk and dresser for his room. It was my joy to clear spaces and make room in our life for the talented Korean man whom Tim and I had already welcomed into our hearts.

For many years, I envisioned converting our garage-attic space into a room with a stairway to replace the pull-down attic ladder. Carrying boxes up the narrow wooden ladder through the small opening became less safe with time. With the gift of an inheritance after the passing of my mother and the help of a structural engineer and contractor, I fulfilled my vision and created a room that became Jinho's music studio.

A longing fulfilled is sweet to the soul...
— Proverbs 13:19

I was pleased with the attic transformation and loved gifting Jinho with his studio when he returned to Oregon. He eventually filled the space with two sets of drums, a piano, a synthesizer, a composer's desk with four screens, an electronic keyboard, computers, books,

CDs, and more. He has loved it. Like the woman who poured her precious oil on Jesus's feet, I poured out my best for one whom God loved so much that I believed He sent me to Korea to meet him.

On Jinho's first Christmas in Oregon, my family came to celebrate. We watched old 8 mm family movies that our dad had taken. The vintage reels featured several Christmases from our childhood. In one home movie, I watched three-year-old "Linda Lou." I got emotional when I saw myself, as a little girl, affectionately hugging my stuffed elephant and giving my baby doll tender kisses. I was already holding and nurturing a "baby" in my arms.

It touched my heart to see that my gentle mothering nature was already present at such a young age. But that sweet young Linda would grow up and never be able to have or hold her own baby. Though I had the expectation that I might want to bring a cute Korean child home with me, I never imagined having the opportunity to share the life and dreams of a warmhearted, gifted Korean man.

What a joy it has been to hear beautiful music flowing from Jinho. When he has played the piano, I have sometimes felt sad places in my heart being healed. When I was touched by Jinho's musical gift, I told him I felt his "David anointing." Young David in the Bible played music for the tormented King Saul, which brought relief to the king's agony. Jinho has touched hearts through his music, too. When Professor Tom, the head of the WOU music department, retired last year, he gave Jinho his conducting baton. Written on the baton it said, "King David" — a special confirmation of Jinho's anointing.

Being connected to one of God's sons has allowed me to experience the kind of special moments I was previously denied. On our drives to school, I delighted in cloud-filled skies as we talked about hundreds of things. We have listened to inspired music and watched many great movies, as he studied their beautiful musical scores. We made a mess of the kitchen with our extravagant cooking sessions; we blended east-west cuisine, and I developed my chopstick skills. Some of life's simplest moments have brought me the greatest joys. We have laughed, and danced, and sang a lot. At times, it seemed we'd been cut from the same cloth.

I never experienced a child's "terrible twos," a teen's acne and puberty, or being able to help a young daughter build her self-esteem. I have, however, been privileged to enjoy life with a gifted musician. We have shared our histories, blended cultures, and discussed art, movies, and faith. We fed the neighbor's goats and breathed in nature on our country walks. Tim and I have listened to Jinho's musical compositions, film scores, and concert performances. We shared traveling adventures in Korea, Oregon, Washington, California, and picturesque Italy. I have listened with my heart when Jinho talked. He has taught me many interesting things, and I have helped him with his English. Our plus-one life together has been richly blessed, even doubly blessed as we have witnessed by double egg yolks in the frying pan and double rainbows in our country skies.

It has been my privilege to celebrate Jinho and to be his prayer warrior. I have contended for his destiny as we faced life's challenges together. He is a special, one-of-a-kind individual who marches to the beat of his own drum. I do not remember wanting the success of another person as much as I have his. I have considered it a privilege to share life with Jinho and to champion his destiny. And he has championed mine.

I praise you because I am fearfully and wonderfully made;
your works are wonderful; I know that full well.
— Psalm 139:14

I have enjoyed loving and encouraging a unique, multi-talented creative individual. It is both a privilege and a responsibility to support those who are placed in our life and entrusted to our heart. When I wondered if my love would be enough, I remembered that meeting Jinho was part of the plan. When he has worn the burgundy sweater I saw on him in my vision six months before we met, I have been reminded that it was God's plan for our paths to intersect.

Of all the women on this planet, I received the invitation to go to Korea to love a nation and its people. When I said, "Yes," I also got to be the one to meet Jinho. I highly value musicians and creative people. I am one of them. I have always believed that each of us should pursue what we love doing. Jinho definitely has a talent and a love for music. I hope he will continue to pursue and thrive in what he is most passionate about. At the end of wise King Solomon's life, he came to this conclusion:

A man can do nothing better than to eat and drink
and find satisfaction in his work.
— Ecclesiastes 2:24

Destiny has always been an important matter to me. Many times, I have wondered, "What if I had not said, 'Yes' to my invitation to go to Korea?" When I seized my opportunity, a positive domino effect began to occur. My obedience opened the way for Jinho to come to America to study composition and media music. Those who know Jinho understand that he is a gift. I was not expecting Jinho, and he was not anticipating me. Through God's loving design and timing, we were connected. I am continually in awe and thankful of how our journey together came to be.

I never knew how enjoyable it could be to share life with a musician. The world needs fresh, inspired music, and talented musicians need the appreciation and support of us all. Throughout time, when creativity flowed from those who were anointed, healing came, and more inspired works were birthed. May this world explode with the anointing of my Creator.

"And from this windowpane, the world seems like a dream.
The lights shine on these streets where you and I have been.
Sometimes I think I see you looking back at me.
To a place where I was safe when the world felt like a knife
Loving you has been the best part of my life."
—Marc Jordan

Thank you, Jesus, for your constant, unfailing love.

Song: *"Best Part of My Life," by Marc Jordan*

43.
JINHO'S STORY

Jinho learned from a young age that there was great joy in creating something. When he was three years old, his mother was a choir member at her church. While she attended her practice, Jinho played in the church sandbox. He found a way to spend time as he enjoyed creating trains, castles, and animals with the sand. During his playtime, Jinho felt a soft, warm breeze coming from the forest behind the church. That was the first time he became aware of God's presence. He felt God encountering him, and he knew He would take care of him.

Jinho loved music, long before we were a part of his life. When he was only five years old, South Korean Jinho began taking piano lessons. At that same time, his Korean mother took him to movies like Steven Spielberg's E.T. (1982) and Roland Joffe's The Mission (1986). He loved the dreamy experience in the dark theatre. While listening to Vangelis's score in Chariots of Fire (1981) when he was seven, he learned how music elevated the drama of motion pictures. He also listened to a film-music radio program when he was a sixth-grader and was captivated by the wonder of motion pictures and the musical scores written by composers like Ennio Morricone and Hans Zimmer.

His musical tastes were versatile and mature for his young age. When he was only eleven, Jinho saw Miles Davis' album Kind of Blue in a record-store window, made his purchase, and then fell in love with jazz. He also listened to and watched American Armed Forces radio and TV programs in Korea that featured jazz, alternative rock, R&B, and many other genres of music. One of the midnight television programs he liked to watch was *The Sunday Art Stage* (일요예술무대) from MBC, which featured musicians that were graduates of the well-respected Berklee College of Music in Boston, Massachusetts.

At thirteen years of age, Jinho began to compose on his piano, and he dreamed that one day he could attend Berklee, too. Music was what he always felt most passionate about. His Korean parents sent him to a variety of academies and schools in an attempt to get him into the best colleges and guide him into practical employment. Jinho was focused, however, on his musical interests and spent his teens and twenties writing, arranging jazz and pop music, performing, and teaching drums. It seemed he was born for music.

When Jinho was thirty-one years of age, he finally got to attend the Berklee College of Music in Boston. He was planted in rich soil and was privileged to study music with other passionate and talented musicians and composers from around the world. After an eighteen-year wait, Jinho finally achieved one of his dreams and graduated from Berklee in 2013 as a drum-performance major. He also studied film scoring for a year after graduation.

Following his season at Berklee, he returned to Korea and hoped that musical opportunities would open up for him. The competition among young and talented musicians in Korea is intense, however, and Jinho did not have as many opportunities to perform or compose as he had hoped. He did play regularly at his church and went to weekly jazz jam sessions, where he received compliments from other musicians. He did not quit on his dream, and he continued practicing and pursuing his music.

In the summer of 2016, while he was playing drums in his rented practice room, Jinho questioned his future and wondered how he could support himself through his music. He was ripe for a divine intervention. At that same time, a lady in Oregon received a vision of Jinho and began to pray for him. I was that lady. I felt led to pray for Jinho before I even met him.

With Tim's support, I went from America to Korea, where Jinho and I met. I felt privileged to be sent into his life at a time when he needed affirmation and encouragement for his musical talents and dreams. We eventually sponsored him as he pursued his Master's degree in composition and film scoring. We were proud when Jinho's hard work awarded him a Master's degree with summa cum laude honors. Music is his true passion and his gifting.

We have celebrated who Jinho is — a gifted musician and caring person. We have cheered him on as he pursued his musical dreams and his life goals. He has eyes that see the beauty in the world around him and ears to create the melodies that accompany what he sees. There is no doubt that Jinho was born for music. He wants to touch people's hearts with his inspired creations. His music has definitely touched my heart.

I once asked his accomplished composition professor, Dr. Kevin Walczyk, "How can we best support Jinho as a composer?" He told me that we were already doing the most important thing by loving him. Then he added, "And get him out of his studio and into nature, where he will be inspired." And so, we are. We have visited oceans, rivers, lakes, and mountains and enjoyed the rich beauty of the Pacific Northwest. We have also gone to the concerts of some of Jinho's and my favorite composers at venues like Seattle, Washington's Jazz Alley, and other concert halls in Portland and Eugene, Oregon, to hear musicians like: Jacob Collier, Dave Grusin, Bob James, Gregoire Maret, Branford Marsalis, Pat Metheny, Danillo Perez, Chris Porter, Lee Ritenour, and Maria Schneider, just to name a few. We have also watched dozens of inspiring movies.

A musical highlight was when we traveled all the way to Italy in the summer of 2018 to see Italian composer Ennio Morricone conduct one of his final concerts. The stunning event was held in the gorgeous ancient setting of the Baths of Caracalla (AD 212 and 216-17). What an amazing evening we shared with Ennio's adoring fans in his hometown of Rome! It was a night I wished would never end — *la dolce vita!*

This journey we were given to share has been a memorable one. We are thankful for the many blessings of this life. May our adventure continue and love keep flowing. We hope to touch the world through our faith, beautiful musical creations, and inspired storytelling. We have regularly asked for the inspiration to create, the wisdom to find our path, and the best doors to our destinies to open.

The good work He has begun in all of us He will complete. God has been so faithful and generous with us. I am so thankful for our journey with Jinho, and I marvel at how the miraculous motion picture of our lives has been directed. I am confident that Jinho will continue to create beautiful music.

Three of Jinho's favorites songs:

Song: *"Dream of the Return," by Pat Metheny Group*

Song: *"10,000 Miles," by Mary Chapin Carpenter*

Video: *Type keywords, "Sanctuary by Jinho" on Youtube.*
Dedicated to Linda. www.youtu.be/R8ZpKAmYhv4

44.
A THOUSAND
SLEEPLESS NIGHTS

Infertility is a silent suffering. Studies show that almost half of those who have grieved from infertility consider it the most upsetting event in their lives. Their barrenness has caused emotions like depression, hopelessness, anger, jealousy, and resentment. We barren women have sometimes doubted that we really were "fearfully and wonderfully made." We questioned our significant relationships because we thought that the love we wanted was supposed to bear fruit — mainly children and a happy family life. We feared for our future, and we sometimes felt completely inadequate to make our lives turn out the way we wanted them to.

We have been guilty of quietly, even defiantly, shaking our fist at the One who created us and who promised there was a future and a hope stored up for us. We have been comforted to hear that these experiences were common among us and to learn that our Creator accepted us right in the middle of our messy struggles. We cried, and complained, and we even doubted Him. We have spent a thousand sleepless nights asking our questions, often receiving no answers. He was, and still is, big enough to handle every emotion we expressed.

Looking back, I can see how alone I felt in my private pain. Though a few people prayed for me through the years, I eventually became too disheartened to go forward at healing services for prayer. There were times when prayer was offered at church services for infertile couples and women who wanted babies. Part of me wanted to receive prayer, even after I passed my self-appointed, fortieth-year baby deadline. I remember turning to my husband and asking him, "Am I supposed to go get prayer?" The time came when I was unsure what I should want.

Tim says he knows that infertility consumed our lives, but that is about all he remembers. I have no memory of talking to him during the day about wanting a baby or questioning my purpose. There was a season when I was home alone, lying on the couch, suffering with chronic fatigue, as my menstrual cycle gradually slowed to a stop. I think my body became too exhausted to go through its monthly routine. Those were the days when a whirlwind of emotions threatened to consume me. I was no longer a talented woman who juggled many exciting tasks simultaneously. My lifeless body and mind could only be still. Resting was about all I could manage.

I do not remember having meaningful conversations with my parents about feeling sad because I was not a mom. I really had no indications they were disappointed in me for not producing a grandchild for them, but I assumed that, somehow, I had failed to fulfill their hopes, too. It was my own imagination that carried my heart and mind to unhealthy places.

I wanted to create cute rooms for the babies and children who never came. I never did get to decorate a nursery for a baby. Some of you have experienced the pain of preparing a room for a baby that never came, or an infant who left too soon. I can only imagine the depth of your pain. I am deeply sorry for your loss.

I was unable to express to others how broken and inadequate I felt as an infertile woman. Even at church, where we declared, "God is good, all the time," I wondered why, if he was always so good, my baby never came. I wondered if, somehow, I had even disappointed God. I did not share my darkest thoughts or my emotional vulnerabilities with many others.

People may have thought, and even suggested, that infertile women should just pull themselves together and move on with their lives. When I was struggling with depression, a member of my extended family said to me, "Get yourself up!" I can tell you, that kind of exhortation did nothing to lift my spirit or bring healing to my wounded heart. Unless you are one who has been, or may still be infertile, you simply cannot understand that infertility is not something a woman can just get over. For me, infertility was an unchangeable reality that had to be walked out, one emotional step at a time. Through the various seasons of my life, the emotions my infertility caused continually resurfaced and demanded that I deal with them. There is no way around some experiences in life.

> *"The best way out is always through."*
> — *Robert Frost*

We have all struggled with barrenness in our lives of one kind or another. It is said that, "Time is a healer." I have found that to be mostly true. Even though there are heartbreaking times and memories we will never forget, we discovered that a key to our surviving was to choose how we let our unchangeable condition and the events of our lives impact us and affect our future.

In time, I moved on from my own deep disappointment to the acceptance of my "childless" status. I gradually transitioned from the death of my vision to the hope of a brighter day. As a woman of faith,

I began to trust that things would eventually work out for my good. "Eventually" was a long time in coming.

There was a time when I realized there was more to me than the labels "infertile," "childless," and "barren." For me, the process of resignation and acceptance was just that, a process, and not a defeat. I opened my heart and my life up to new possibilities. I released everything that my hand had a tight grip on; I let Him take out and put in whatever He thought was best. Opportunities eventually came that redefined my identity. Thankfully, I had the faith to believe that there was a hopeful, fruitful future ahead for me. That belief was not something I manufactured — it was simply a gift of faith.

A few years ago, Canadian researchers looked at women in their sixties and seventies who had struggled with infertility when they were younger. A third of the women eventually had biological children, a third had adopted, and a third remained childless. Interestingly, when the researchers examined the women, they found that their psychological profiles were identical. They were all equally happy and had survived their infertility just fine.

I am thankful to have known many childless women and couples who have survived — even thrived — in their childlessness. Some had decided not to have children and lived rich, meaningful lives. Like me, others were unable to have children. Even though I did not get the life I had wanted, thankfully I made it through my place of barrenness to the fulfillment of a fruitful life. I came to believe that no matter what the outcome would be, there were blessings ahead for us all.

Song: "Blessings," by Laura Story

Thank you, Jaeyoung and Younghee, for your beautiful gifts.
아름다운 선물 보내주셔서 감사드립니다.

45.
A LONGING FULFILLED

When my faith was tested, I trusted God. I had received His many "kisses" and seen too much of His love to doubt or give up on my life. I held on, even when it felt like I was hanging on by just a thread. In Matthew 17:20, it says, "If you have faith as small as a mustard seed, you can say to this mountain, 'Move from here to there,' and it will move. Nothing will be impossible for you." Just a seed of faith is all we need to move mountains; nothing will be impossible for us. I can say, with a grateful heart, that I always had at least a small mustard seed of faith. Faith did eventually move my mountains.

While writing this book, I reflected on the highs and lows of my journey through infertility and childlessness. I remembered feeling unknown, even invisible, to the women around me. I never qualified for active membership in "The Moms Club." There was no baby stroller in the back of my minivan or Parent-Teacher Association meetings to attend. I had no child's school pictures in my wallet or "World's Best Mom" magnet holding my children's artwork on the refrigerator. My calendar was void of the events like Soccer-Mom Saturdays, birthday parties, and family trips to the zoo, the beach, and Disneyland. I have not seen all the Disney movies, and I cannot sing all the words to Idina Menzel's popular song, "Let It Go." There were many times I felt like an alien in a gathering of moms, and I kept silent in the midst of their conversations. I just never got plugged in to the everyday life of a mom.

Hell in the Hallway

As it forced me to reflect back upon my years of memories, writing this book has been a cathartic experience. Many times, I had pondered the saying, "When one door closes, another one opens," but there is usually a hallway between the two doors. And it can be hell in the hallway. The hallway was my place of intense uncertainty, when life as I hoped for had died, and what was to come was still a mystery. I felt thankful again that no matter how many times I became disappointed, disheartened, or felt utterly alone, I found the strength to press on. I received new insights and broken places in my heart were healed.

> *God is within her; she will not fall...*
> *— Psalm 46:5*

In spite of the reality of my permanent infertility and the years of questioning my future, I received enough inspiration and motivation to live an otherwise fruitful and productive life. When my "Plan A" was eliminated, I had the courage to look for my "Plan B" and then my "Plan C." After persevering through my pain, I finally reached the times when breakthroughs came and unexpected surprises finally showed up. My miracle did not come after waiting in hopeful anticipation and then finally getting pregnant. I learned to live an otherwise passionate and fruitful life without ever receiving my miracle baby. Life itself, and whatever experiences that came, were themselves the miracles.

Each part of my journey, the opportunities, the choices, the failures, and the victories — they were all part of life. As I wrote, I reflected on all of it. It now seems miraculous to me that I even lived to see the time of fulfillment I was born for. I did not get permanently stuck in my pain, even though disappointments and grief did threaten to take me out. I endured the ups and downs of life's roller coaster ride. My hope may have been deferred, delayed, and redefined, but it was not denied. When fog settled in around me and I could not see my hand in front of my face, I somehow imagined that happier days were ahead.

To those who are experiencing barrenness in your life, I say, "There will be fruitfulness." To the infertile women and childless couples reading this book, I pray you will feel encouraged and hopeful. Though this is just one woman's journey, more importantly, it is the testimony of a faithful Father God. I wish I had the power to grant the desires of your hearts for a child or for your dreams to come true — I really do. But I am not the "Author and finisher of your faith" — He is. We each have our own unique path to travel. You cannot imagine what He might put on your path!

Life will not always be easy. It is OK to feel upset when your friends announce their pregnancy or you watch as someone else's dream is being fulfilled. While I was writing this book, three women I know announced they were pregnant with girls. They had all experienced heartaches and struggles; one woman was infertile, and two others lost their babies, one a son and the other a daughter. I realized again the importance of celebrating with women who finally received the desire of their hearts. As you wait in hopeful anticipation, allow yourself to experience your emotions, even the most difficult ones like anger, hopelessness, and the pain of rejection or betrayal.

If your story is not unfolding as you hoped it would, remember that it is not finished yet. Ask for the courage to persevere, despite the obstacles you may be facing. Your struggle will become a part of your story. Be a warrior and fight back the doubts that threaten to steal your faith. Hold onto trust, and believe that good things are on the way. Be open to blessings in whatever form they may come. Life often looks different than what we expected.

> *"You are so hard on yourself. Take a moment. Sit back.*
> *Marvel at your life:*
> *at the grief that softened you,*
> *at the heartache that made you wise,*
> *at the suffering that strengthened you.*
> *Despite everything, you still grew. Be proud of this."*
> *— Anonymous*

Live out your own story, every single line and chapter, every scene. Stay open to new opportunities, and enjoy each moment for what it offers. Life is a gift! Pursue your own dreams. Do not be limited by the expectations or control of others. Avoid the trap of comparing yourself to others. "Success" is living the life YOU are called to live. Do not waste your time on negative thoughts or speech. Plan to look back on your life someday with no regrets, believing you made good decisions and had positive expectations. Let yourself be stirred up about what He is calling YOU to do. Go where He leads. Do as He says, whenever He nudges you to do it.

Whatever may be going on in or around you, keep praying and

praising through it all. Do your best to choose healthy responses to the stuff of life. Do not medicate your anxiety or your grief, but confess your addictions and get free, whatever it takes. And stay free. Kill worrying and keep yourself in the place of peace.

Pray that you will be led into the right relationships and out of the destructive ones. Look for the people who will champion your identity and celebrate who you are, and invite them into your life. Ask that you will recognize when to break free from the people who are users or those who are unworthy of your support. Stay close to your supporters.

I know that heartaches can tenderize you and that hard times will make you wiser. All your suffering is meant to strengthen you as you continue to grow and become. Allow yourself to be pruned. Even rose bushes must be aggressively trimmed to produce an abundance of gorgeous roses. Your greatest pain can produce the most power in your life and will become the platform that you tell your story from. The book you are holding in your hands is proof of that truth. I promise you, none of your life lessons or experiences will be wasted. If you are still on this planet breathing, you are being prepared for a hopeful future that is yet to come.

As you wait in eager anticipation for a baby, a miracle to happen in your life, or to receive a vision for your uncertain future, may you experience that life itself is also a miracle. What is coming may just be better than you could have ever asked or imagined it would be. Stay open to life — your life. Here is the happy ending I promised you in Chapter One:

I have a purpose, and I am walking out my destiny!

I am a lover of God, a prayer warrior, one who is going to the nations, and a champion of one of Korea's special, creative men. Against all odds, and in spite of what I experienced or how I felt, I held onto hope. You can, too. I reached the place where the desires of my heart were, and still are, being fulfilled. I believe the best is yet to come. We can all see God fulfill His purposes for us. I have books to write and dreams to spark. (Just last week, in June of 2020, my friend Ivan prophesied to me that I was a "Mother of Nations.") Tim has people to meet and encourage. Jinho has things to discover, talents to develop, and music to create. There are more countries to visit and people around the world waiting to experience His love.

Do not underestimate your potential. Allow yourself to be blessed. When you find yourself living between bold, courageous faith and crippling fear, press on. Believe you are who He says you are. More importantly, trust in whose you are. Seek truth, and be a communicator of His Truth. Dare to believe that you can bless the world — and go do it. Bring the gift of YOU wherever you are led. Believe in the Author of happy endings.

Sing, barren woman, you who never bore a child,
burst into song, shout for joy, you who were never
in labor, because more are the children of the desolate
woman than of her who has a husband, says the Lord.
— Isaiah 54:1

Song: "The Legend of 1900," by Ennio Morricone

A PRAYER FOR THE EPHESIANS AND YOU

For this reason, I kneel before the Father, from whom every family in heaven and on earth derives its name. I pray that out of his glorious riches he may strengthen you with power through his Spirit in your inner being, so that Christ may dwell in your hearts through faith. And I pray that you, being rooted and established in love, may have power, together with all the Lord's holy people, to grasp how wide and long and high and deep is the love of Christ, and to know this love that surpasses knowledge — that you may be filled to the measure of all the fullness of God. Now to him who is able to do immeasurably more than all we ask or imagine, according to his power that is at work within us, to him be glory in the church and in Christ Jesus throughout all generations, for ever and ever! Amen.
— Ephesians 3:14-21

Song: "I'll Lead You Home," by Michael W. Smith

BLESSINGS

BY LAURA STORY

We pray for blessings.
We pray for peace.
Comfort for family, protection while we sleep
We pray for healing, for prosperity
We pray for your mighty hand to ease our suffering.
All the while, you hear each spoken need.
Yet love is way too much to give us lesser things.

'Cause what if your blessings come through raindrops?
What if your healing comes through tears?
What if a thousand sleepless nights are what it takes to know you're near?
What if trials of this life are your mercies in disguise?

We pray for wisdom
Your voice to hear
We cry in anger when we cannot feel you near.
We doubt your goodness; we doubt your love,
As if every promise from your word is not enough.
All the while, you hear each desperate plea
And long that we'd have faith to believe.

When friends betray us
When darkness seems to win
We know that pain reminds this heart
That this is not our home.

What if my greatest disappointments
Or the aching of this life
Are the revealing of a greater thirst this world can't satisfy?
What if trials of this life
The rain, the storms, the hardest nights
Are your mercies in disguise?

SONG AND VIDEO LIST

A playlist is available via Google "Linda SBW playlist."

Thank you, Jesus
Song: "Goodness of God" (Lyrics), sung by Jenn Johnson, YT.
Written by Ed Cash, Ben Fielding, Jason Ingram, Brian Johnson, and Jenn Johnson.

Chapter One — Dreams Really Do Come True
Song: "Somewhere Over the Rainbow," sung by Eva Cassidy, YT.
Original song: written by Yip Harburg.

Chapter Two — Life in Redwood City
Song: "The Story of Arirang," YT.
Created by the Korean Traditional Culture and Art Foundation.
Song: "So Hyang — Arirang Alone" | 소향 – 아리랑 [Immortal Songs 2], YT
Written by Hadol, arranged by Hwang Seongje, based on the Korean traditional folk song, "Arirang."

Chapter Five — A Future and a Hope
Song: "The Prayer," by Andrea Bocelli and Katharine McPhee (Live 2008), YT.
Written by David Foster, Tony Renis, Carole Bayer Sager, and Alberto Testa.

Chapter Seven — The Birthing of an Historic Preservationist
Song: "Be Thou My Vision" music video, sung by Audrey Assad, YT.
Based on a poem by sixth-century Irish poet Dallan Forgaill.

Chapter Eleven — Pushing the "Pause" Button
Song: "Perfect Peace," written and sung by Laura Story, YT.
Song: "You Say," written and sung by Lauren Daigel (Official Music Video), YT.
Song: "You Raise Me Up" (Official Music Video), by Josh Groban, YT.
Written by David W. Foster, Toney Renis, Carole Bayer Sager, and Alberto Testa.

Chapter Fourteen — Teamwork
Song: "Legacy," written and sung by Nichole Nordeman, YT.

Chapter Fifteen — A Divine Interruption and a Spiritual Sabbatical
Song: "I'd Rather Have Jesus," sung by Selah, YT.
Written by Oscar C.A. Bernadotte.
Song: "Lord Let Your Glory Fall," written and sung by Matt Redman, YT.

Chapter Sixteen — Return to a Changing World
Song: "I Will Carry You", written and sung by Michael W. Smith, YT.

SONG AND VIDEO LIST

Chapter Nineteen — Passing the Baton
Song: "Faithful," by Amy Renée Miller

Chapter Twenty-One — Floods Will Come
Song: "With a Little Help From My Friends," by The Beatles, YT.
Written by John Lennon and Paul McCartney.

Chapter Twenty-Two — Merry Crashmas
A Divine Interruption: testimony by Michael W. Smith, YT.

Chapter Twenty-Six — Praying for the Famous
Song: "Perhaps Love," written and sung by John Denver.
Live at the Apollo Theatre (1982), YT.

Chapter Thirty-Five — My Mother's Challenging Season
Song: "Blank Stares," written and sung by Jay Allen (Official Music Video), YT.

Chapter Thirty-Six — Called to Go
Song: "The Mission" (Main Theme), composed by Ennio Morricone, YT.
The film: The Mission, Directed by Roland Joffe, starring Robert De Niro and Jeremy Irons.

Chapter Thirty-Seven — Maiden Voyage to Korea
Song: "Oceans," sung by Taya Smith with Hillsong, YT.
Written by Michael Guy Chislett, Matt Crocker, Joel Houston, and Salomon Lightheim.
Hillsong UNITED, 2003.

Chapter Thirty-Eight — Carried by Prayer
Song: "Wind Beneath My Wings," by Bette Midler, YT.
Written by Larry Henley and Jeff Silbar.
Song: "Great Are You, Lord (Live)," sung by Casting Crowns, YT.
Written by Jason Ingram, David Leonard, and Leslie Jordan.

Chapter Forty — Letters from Korea
Video: Joseph Butso singing gospel songs in downtown Seoul, South Korea, and Joseph Butso,
I Can See Your Voice 3.
Song: "Good Good Father," written and sung by Chris Tomlin.
Song: "Amazing Grace (My Chains Are Gone)," written and sung by Chris Tomlin.
Song: "Well Done," written and sung by The Afters.
Song: "Reckless Love" (Live with story), written and sung by Cory Asbury,
Bethel Church, Heaven Come 2017.

SONG AND VIDEO LIST

Song: *"Memory of the Wind," by Naul (바람추억)*
Video: Seoul Wave, filmed and directed by Brandon Li.
Video: Seungyeol Lee — main theme song from the K-Drama, Incomplete Life.

Chapter Forty-One — Our Adventure Continues
Song: "Best Part of My Life," written and sung by Marc Jordan, YT.

Chapter Forty-Three — Jinho's Story
Song: "Dream of the Return," by Pat Metheny Group, YT.
Composed by Pat Metheny with Lyle Mays on piano, lyrics written and sung by Pedro Aznar.
Song: "10,000 Miles," sung by Mary Chapin Carpenter, YT.
Composed by Mark Isham, based on an 18th-century English folk ballad, featured in the movie Fly Away Home (1996), directed by Carroll Ballard.
Video: "Sanctuary" by Jinho Choi (2019), YT. Dedicated to Linda.

Chapter Forty-Four — A Longing Fulfilled
Song: "The Legend of 1900," composed by Ennio Morricone, YT.
A Prayer for the Ephesians and You
Song: "I'll Lead You Home," written and sung by Michael W. Smith, YT.

The Lyrics to "Blessings" — by Laura Story
Song: "Blessings," written and sung by Laura Story, YT.

Thank you, Columbia Records, for permission to use Laura's lyrics.
I pray her poignant song will bring encouragement to many people.

Do you have a dream?
I'd love to hear about it.

linda.dreamsparker@gmail.com

Made in the USA
Monee, IL
09 March 2022

92442260R00210